ASSARACUS

A Journal of Gay Poetry
Issue 3

Sibling Rivalry Press

Assaracus
A Journal of Gay Poetry
Issue 3: July 2011
ISBN 978-0-9832931-5-6
ISSN 2159-0478
Bryan Borland, Editor
Copyright © 2011 by Sibling Rivalry Press, LLC

Cover Art, "Spencer" by Cody Henslee. Used by Permission. Model, Spencer Smith.

All rights reserved. No part of this journal may be reproduced or republished without written consent from the publisher, except by reviewers who may quote brief excerpts in connection with a review in a newspaper, magazine, or electronic publication; nor may any part of this journal be reproduced, stored in a retrieval system, or transmitted in any form without written consent of the publisher. However, contributors maintain ownership rights of their individual poems and as such retain all rights to publish and republish their work.

Sibling Rivalry Press, LLC
13913 Magnolia Glen Drive
Alexander, AR 72002

www.siblingrivalrypress.com

ASSARACUS

Steven Cordova
p. 6

Terry Jaensch
p. 16

Nicholas YB Wong
p. 29

Scott Wiggerman
p. 40

Carl Miller Daniels
p. 50

Ahimsa Timoteo Bodhrán
p. 66

Chuck Willman
p. 76

Bryan Borland
p. 89

Jeremy Halinen
p. 101

Antler
p. 112

Poems Inspired by James Franco
p. 127

Cover Art by Cody Henslee
Artist's Biography p. 140

CORDOVA
STEVEN

baby, you ain't light

Steven Cordova's first full-length volume of poems, *Long Distance*, appeared in January 2010 from Bilingual Review Press. Forthcoming are a short story in *Ambientes: New Queer Latino Fiction* (University of Wisconsin Press) and an essay in *The Other Latino* (University of Arizona Press).

ON BEAUTY AND THE BEAUTIFUL SEÑOR

The Beautiful *Señor* lives in the shadow of his own beauty just as—you and I—we die in it.

The plain are not to the plain as the beautiful are to the beautiful; the plain are not to the beautiful as the beautiful to the plain. (O My Beautiful *Señor*, I typed "pain.")

Yes, My Beautiful *Señor,* you deserve love as much as I do. You deserve heartbreak, too.

Les beaux artes et les artes utiles—O My Beautiful *Señor*,
you were these things to me.

It is polite to accept a compliment. But My Beautiful *Señor*, *Thou art as wise as thou art beautiful* could simply mean *thou art an ass.*

A cool aesthetic may be beautiful; rarely, if ever, is it hot.

Some faces are meant to remain blank, others to be written upon.

Beauty is truth, truth beauty. But all my beautiful *Señor* tells me are lies.

Beauty may only be skin-deep but it's the blush, if you will—the very firmness of a cheek—we use to decide which apple we really, really want.

Though the sight of The Beautiful *Señor* often leaves me pained, I refrain from tearing out my own eyes. It would be far too ugly an act.

ACROSS A TABLE (SO IT'S LIKE THAT, IS IT?)

"So it's like that, is it?"
"No, it's not like that.

It's like that."
"That's what I said. It's like that."

"Yes, but it's not like that
that. It's like that that."

"And does that make
all the difference?"

"Yes, that makes all the difference.
But only if we agree

on that."

      *

"It's all good."
"Is it? Is it all good?"

"Yes, it's all good."
"Even the murders?

Even the inhumanity of man to man?"
"Well, no, all that's not good."

"So what's good is good
but not all that's good is good?"

"Well, I don't know about that,
man. But whatever it is, you've got it.

You've got it good."

DARKER LIMERICKS

There was a young man named Perdition.
Perdition was always on a mission.
  The buckles would go a-flying
  And soon we'd both a-sighing.
For Perdition I was all submission.

*

If I couldn't let him in the front door
Then I'd let him in the back (some more).
  What his little Mrs. didn't know
  Didn't hurt. And I never said no.
Said, "Please do me, sir, like you did me before."

ACROSS A TABLE (IS EVERYTHING ALRIGHT?)

"Is *everything* alright?"
"Is *everything* ever all alright

all at the same time?"
"Come on, will you

just tell me, is *everything* alright?"
"What is 'everything?'"

"Just *everything*—everything.
Is *everything* alright?"

"You mean *my* everything?"
"Damn it, I just mean *everything*."

"Well, you can't mean *everything*—can you?—
but you must mean *something*."

    *

"Did *something* happen?"
"*Something* is always happening."

"I mean, did *something* happen?"
"You mean did I by chance

happen to do *something*, something
as opposed to the usual nothing?"

"No, I mean did *something* happen?"
"You mean did I happen to happen upon

something?" "Please, did
something happen?"

"Yes, something happened.
But mostly nothing, nothing happened."

GOING

Sometimes I find the only benefit of going
to therapy, of having a friend, is that I no longer
have to bore my therapist-friends.

"I'm only human" is a humanist invention.
Invoked too often, it will bring us to our knees
and the very edge of our humanity.

And perhaps there is pleasure and there is pressure
in going because there is pressure and there is pleasure
in sex. Perhaps between this life of celibacy

and that life of promiscuity there is some other life,
perhaps there is some other man—a man, I mean,
of consequence. A man of action. Though it's true,

such a man and such a dream is often a dream-man
who does not have to suffer the consequences,
not of his own and not of any one else's actions.

I'm smart enough to know I'm not very smart;
loud enough to know I'm not very quiet
and this is why I'll end by saying

that while none of us are alone each of us is alone
in our aloneness. And it smarts. It smarts, this smartness.
Sometimes I find it is the only benefit of going.

ON FIRE ISLAND

Love is the man who braves the sea to retrieve the ball his
        dog won't from anything but the wet, impressionable sands.

Love is the dog who pants, waiting for the man to emerge
        from the sea. The sea seems to go on forever.

Love is the bitter taste of the sea; how, without a fresh
        bucket of water, we die.

Love is the retreating beneath the surface of the sea which
        is, and which cannot be separated from, the sea.

Love is that. Love is all that which will take us out.

SEX AND CELL PHONES

7th Street between First and Second Avenues: A man is on his cell phone pacing the pavement, gesticulating wildly, practically swallowing the phone as he shouts over angry traffic horns, "No, I'm on 7th Street! 7th Street! Between First and Second Avenues!"

    The lily pad lies luxuriously on the pond; the cell phone vibrates in your ear.

"His cell phone is like his dick used to be—he handles it all the time."

"'cept the cell phone gets more action than his dick ever did."

"Mark my words, soon they'll make dildos shaped like cell phones."

    The instruments of sex are hard.

The cell phone has led to the partial death of cruising. It sounds alarmist, I know. But it's true. I passed a man on the street the other day. He was standing beneath an awning which read "Top and Bottoms" (it was a lingerie store). This man was talking on his cell, but he distinctly cruised me as I passed, giving me that deeply serious, piercing look of recognition and carnal need. I slowed down. He kept cruising me. But he couldn't be distracted from his cell-phone conversation fast enough. I walked away. I always walk away.

    "When I'm alone, I want to be alone."

If it comes down to getting hit by a car because I was cruising a guy or getting hit by a car because I was talking on my cell phone, guess which one I'd choose?

    The only thing worse than a person who hates cell phones is a person who hates cell phones but "borrows" other people's.

"A cell phone is, like, something, to do, like, you know, whenever you feel, like, you know, uncomfortable doing whatever it is you're, like, doing: like just walking down the street…. Or chillin' with your friends…. Or like, you know, having sex with your boyfriend."

Whoever the man on 7th Street pacing the pavement is talking to raises his voice, too. He raises it loud enough for passersby to hear, so it's as though he's come through a cell and that he is here, too, pacing—pacing the pavement. "*No!*" he shouts, "*I'm on 7th Street. 7th Street between First and Second Avenues.*"

HICK SONNET

Gettin' hitched?—to you & me that'd only mean the needle
pulled through the eye so tight a body can't never get free.
N' work drag n' wedding drag—they only work
'cause no one'd dress like that if they ain't desperate—
& if they ain't desperate & they ain't lonely,
they're lonely enough. Your Bonnie 'n your Clyde—well
they only seemed romantic cause the bankers ... well, hell,
they didn't. I said, "It's all I can do to take care of myself"

but what I meant was, "It's all I can do not to take care of you."
'N so what if I'd believe a sea-horse comin' round the hill,
drunk on dry land, swearin' it's an only child?
I'd never believe you. No way. Unh-unh.
That black hole's been stuck on flush
ten million light years. And baby, you ain't light.

JAENSCH
TERRY

twink, if you are reading this

Terry Jaensch is an Australian poet/actor and monologist. His first book, *Buoy*, was published in 2001 (FIP) and shortlisted for the Anne Elder Award by the Fellowship of Australian Writers. He has worked as Writer-in-Community, Poetry Editor (*Cordite*), Artist-in-Residence, Dramaturge, Artistic Director of the 2005 Emerging Writers' Festival, poetry teacher, and in a variety of arts/community and local government programming positions. In 2004 he wrote and recorded 15 monologues based on his childhood in a Ballarat orphanage for "Life Matters" ABC Radio—since reworked and performed for theatre as "Orphan's Own Project." He was awarded an Asialink residency in Singapore where he worked collaboratively with poet Cyril Wong. The resulting work, *Excess Baggage & Claim* (transitlounge publishing), was launched in 2007. He has won awards including the Melbourne Poet's Union International Poetry Prize and the Victorian Writers' Centre Poetry Slam and was on the winning team of the Melbourne Writers' Festival Poetry Slam. His work has been anthologized and published in journals both nationally and internationally. He has a background in acting, having studied at the Herbert Berghof Studio and Stella Adler Conservatory in New York.

Terry Jaensch

THE POET ASKS HIS LOVE TO WRITE HIM
After Lorca's "Sonnets of Dark Love"

Twink, if you are reading this ring me, SMS
    abbreviate or I am done for—dun 4 i tel u!
The creek bed is risen, bike path beneath. Two
    days of constant rain, no you'd never guess

it our creek. *If you are reading this ring me*
    ducks and geese disconcert at head height
& swans? Well, one fucked Leda for spite.
    I don't want to be fucked by a swan, please

if you are reading this ring me—or wring
    my neck LOL. Be it on your head if I am
fucked by a swan or God LOL. Texting

LOL grows diffuse the deeper you sink
    & these attendant plastic bags—well
a consumption if you're reading me *twink*?

Terry Jaensch

NIGHT OF SLEEPLESS LOVE
After Lorca's "Sonnets of Dark Love"

When he comes home to roost, I will
    sleep. Until then my laptop will burn
a hole in my thigh or die trying. Turns
    out cocks love preternaturally & well

unpenned, if mine is anything to go by.
    Scrolling up the page, down the page
the cock can draw blood and plumage
    to a head, can *send pics & will reply*

with pics, can ravish its own neck until
    he comes home. Cage free & wireless
the cock is outré, part ether part amyl

beak & wattle, is my heart—fibrillate
    when he comes to roost & all is dawn
all is crow & all downloaded: ejaculate.

Terry Jaensch

THE BELOVED SLEEPS ON THE POET'S BREAST
After Lorca's "Sonnets of Dark Love"

This is no place for the faint of heart
    for *wankers time wasters or softcocks*.
Beloved, this pumping station clocks
    its time once & once only—a lark

cannot be had here. This is the flood
    aortic is the Ark heaving its cargo,
there'll be no peace dove, no land ho
    sea legs, you've them too, touchwood

or will grow a pair seafaring. No wank
    no waste, if need be we'll consume
the other. Beloved *softcocks* break rank

run to mother with their slack compasses—
    all front, no prow. The sea is *genuine*
expects same—man-up or man misalliances.

AIR

Had I but the right cutlery, I could cut it
but in this age of convenience and terror I
am not to be trusted. I've a piece of plastic
I must sharpen with my mind, that presently
tears, no wipes, the hang-dog expression
from the face of our single serve of lasagne.
This is not the end or rather the end as I'd
imagined it, this monochromatic restaurant
with its listless salads and half arsed pasta
bakes, its muzak and families dull as tines
on my fork. Craft taxi and dock, no this is
not the end, it is ends—and interminably so.
This poem wants to do so much, the cutlery
apposite: I am trying to lift love, I am trying.

Terry Jaensch

LETTER FROM SUNGAI BULOH

Emptying an urn half her size of mosquito
larvae and water, the architect's Australian
wife tells me of her husbands sister's suicide.

The family never speak of it; the Japanese
occupation of Singapore the need to keep
her inside—for fear of kidnap. Wrigglers
in their throes she returns the vessel to an

upright position. As I write it now, it is
the conflation of two separate events:
the emptying of an urn, a suicide. One

preceding the other by several days. Days
in which I attend the needs of the kampong
in which I am staying. The shutters closed
for the night, twenty four in all, the house

cat without a lizard's gut to puncture
playfully penetrating my hand. She draws
little or no blood that I can sense, certainly

nothing has reached the page. Truth be told
I'm reeling still—from last Sunday's storm,
I was warned against, 'making calls' in such
apocalyptic circumstances. Some appliances

I have simply refused to turn back on…
P.S. An injured boar roams the property each day
at dusk, the sport and buckshot of adolescent

Malays, men the world over—his wound
localised, his temper not. I know better than
to aggravate that animal with my presence
and so write or lip-sync nightly some titanic

ballad the cat will un-requite. Wishing
you were here, wishing you weren't here
the urn, the suicide—love: a conflation.

BUMBOAT TO PULAU UBIN

Into the wind, three Buddhist monks'
garments railing against each wearer's
composure as we approach this small
satellite, this Sentosa waiting to happen.

All eyes keening to our approach. How
zen, our vessel signals not only arrival
but means to departure. The monks
alight first, seemingly without rising

having slummed it across the water—
a show of humility? I've more trouble,
my feet arc at the gap between bow
and pier, the drop, the nothingness

between one thing and another, and
the "too much information" of a starved
dog's almost exoskeletal body: floating.
How you would love it here, the absence

of cars, ATM's, people—in places—save
those that work here. Houses left to their
own devices, shrines too—the equity. No
technology Lords it over (my camera in

its case), no vassals, no fealty but to
our imaginations. Can it last, this romance
this equidistance, this island whose sides
we can accomplish in five minutes or less?

Terry Jaensch

CALLING HOME

> *"Time is the longest distance between two places"*
> *- Tennessee Williams*

Declarations of love and my voice growing fainter,
you ask why I'm so eager to end the conversation.
I've one ear on traffic, the other on the receiver
both anticipating a break in the flow of things.

My feet teeter on the kerb, the metal cord connecting
us fully extended, rod-like, our talk has become punitive.
I'm about to run or not, set something other than my
body in motion or not, though I'm pressed to reason

any desire in stasis. I've not the stance for answers
today, I draw breath and from the action, need
but say nothing of it. A security guard motions
at me from the concrete rim of a flower bed,

his message visible but silent, cannot be got at this
distance: the flowers also arrive, poor travelers,
more or less, certainly—thirsting. Caught between
the mall and the street two Tamil tailors, who later

attempt a garment from my necessary indifference
to them, lock hands. This is love or not—thumbing
the buttons, gesturing—and it will call again before
it leaves; while there's still money on the card.

Terry Jaensch

CLEANING THE APARTMENT

With the venetians drawn we can see the cobwebs
    clinging, you hurry to the kitchen and I bury myself
in a corner, trying to pull something from a window
    recess: a dead spider, a palsied hand. In six years is
it possible we never tended to this spot? The cutlery
    rattles as you remove it from its tray, separating it
into two sets of four. I follow your count as I mop
    the lounge, the bathroom, even the front door-step
I've never held time so well or cared so much that
    something be clean. In the bedroom we contemplate
a flattened lampshade neither of us seems willing
    to commit to—to discard or reinstate. The feature
wall, or as you once referred to it 'a night without
    stars,' dominates now the bed is gone. Half heartedly
we discuss painting it over, this fancy we might now
    pay for with our bond. 'Fuck it, we've done enough.'
It's difficult not to be touched by this, this moment
    of decisiveness that for last traces moves, room
to room. I wring out the mop-head, and startle the
    neighbour's cat with an awkward exit, laden with
garbage bags and cleaning product I can't see one
    foot in front of the other; until now he has ignored
us completely. As we drive to the Brotherhood I rest
    my hand on your knee, palm up: dead spider pulled
from a recess. You spread its legs with your own—
    the car's interior a flood of chemicals—radiating.

FAGGOT (REVIEW)

…that's what he calls me as I leave the cinema. After the shock of its opening, his mouth closes its curtains on a single credit, makes for the exit: from beginning to end there's nothing to substantiate its action. No mise-en-scène supports no exposition suggests no precursory dialogue assists with the thatch of twigs burning by films end. Ill-timed, ill-conceived: cinematically lacking in scope. Script: poor, under-written, overstated, assaults audience with its ignorance. This reviewer was not entertained by its violence. Formulaic, cliché, one could produce it with no thought at all. "Homophobia" no stars, now playing on the smallest screen in the multiplex: his son.

HAGGLING AT CLARKE QUAY

I keep my humour
        the proprietor his—

jovial but firm.
        The joke an antiquity,

punch-line a rumour.
        The Quay plainly put:

bent at this juncture.
        More aesthete than buyer

the argument's won
        in looking farther

afield. Or flattering
        his smoking gun—

drawn from cloth,
        dust jacket cracking:

"Singapore boobies,"
        jaundiced early eighties

erotica. More aesthete
        than buyer I ask after

Mao-ist propaganda.
        Despotic kitsch, busts

and pins I should care
        less about, nor humour.

He starts at twenty,
        I work my way down

—jovial but firm—
        something of my taste

for the "early eighties"
        in Mao's receding hair-line.

KARAOKE - BABYLON

He's not exactly speaking my language, eyeing
himself in the side-board mirror. Sticky rice
queen slumming it, not exactly singing—to me.

His face, the choreographed collective of the duo
on screen, signing its availability to already
established markets. Pre-pubescent mandarin

breaking into even more underdeveloped English:
ooh baby, baby. For all his grasp, its perfunction—
open the window. *Ooh open the window, aah open*

the window. Someone else's standard in a bar filled
with mirrors, singletted, tank topped, body shirted like
so much peanut flesh encased in shell. He holds the mic

like a phallus, my gaze for like—seconds, as the room
choruses ad lib to fade: will any of us have a career
beyond thirty, will any of us have a career beyond thirty?

KARAOKE (KTV CHAIN)

All those standards that engage
the moon's pull at intervals
later refrain. In the park love
dimly but organically lit: tumescent

shadow against my thigh. Young
ah beng who earlier sang of want
of need; so acclimated to the heat
in things as to render his passion

benign, does not act for all he can
observe. Counts himself cliché
amongst the greenery and does not
bay for all baying alerts. We lust

in a Nanny State. His inclinations
crescent and not full. Confucian
ideal: the aria that in opera swells
pop fells, infantilises, perambulates.

WONG
NICHOLAS YB

all eyes can be blinded

Nicholas YB Wong is the author of *Cities of Sameness* (Desperanto, forthcoming) and the winner of several awards, including the *Sentinel Quarterly* Poetry Competition. He also received nominations for the Best of the Net and Web Anthologies in 2010. His poems have appeared in *Lambda Literary, San Pedro River Review, Third Wednesday, The Q Review, Mascara Literary Review, Cha, The Nervous Breakdown, The Medulla Review*, and elsewhere. He is currently a poetry editor for *THIS Literary Magazine* and a poetry reader for *Drunken Boat*.

nicholasybwong.weebly.com

PROTÉGÉ OF THE LADY

What words, then, if you love me,
what beauty not to be sustained
will separate finally dancer from dance.
         - Robert Creeley

Every gay man knows the gaydar was invented
By the Dalai Lama in Uganda in 1986, the same year
Stefani was born in. When she was 5, she put
A toy poodle above her head and wore her
Mother's apron as a tube top, singing and swinging
Her body on the couch. She knew the kitchen
Wasn't her place. She knew the brown curly canine
Mane would speak, as a wig, to the gaydar in a secret
Code understood telepathically by one-
Tenth of the world's population. In her college days,
Influenced by gurus like Roland Barthes
And Jacques Derrida, she decided to call herself
Lady Gaga. Four simple syllables that resemble
A baby talk. A name that you now glorify under the spinning
And glistening mirror ball. She needs not your approval
Or understanding. She doesn't even care if you speak
English. All she seeks is your moves, your body language,
The drifting of your arms in the discotheque music,
Like fallen leaves flowing down the stream, suddenly
Revived by the momentum of the moment. Whether
You're 25 or 55, single or married-but-turned-gay,
Once in love or unloved by someone, she commands you,
With her thick digitalized voice, to dance along the heavy
Beats, the subliminal rah rah ah ah ah roma roma ma
Gaga ooh la la. And you listen, believe and imitate.
You wear on your work-worn poker face a masquerade
And tell yourself you're the queen of this place.
A place where you nearly kneel to worship this diva,
A place whose beauty comes from who you are, a place
Where you turn off your gaydar, as it's already conquered
By who we are.

DAVID AUSTRALIAN

wasn't his real name. Our conversation didn't go
that far. He introduced himself as David in an accent
that I thought was British. "I'm from Australia," he
corrected at once, as if the mistake, to both
of us, was a national shame. In the low-flung street
light outside Zoo (especially after a few shooters),
every gay, be he a Caucasian or a Chinese, looked
beast-like, always on the hunt. In distance, I mistook
him as Mark Doty: a bald head, a tall nose, an oval
face, but of course, lacking the poet's aura. My sight
degenerated, finding all white faces indistinctive.
My doctor said it's a disease common in Hong Kong,
clinically known as Anti-colonialism. The whites
weren't smart either. "Are you a Stanford graduate?"
he asked, fooled by the red fonts on my vanity
tee. "I wish," I said. Then he did the background
check, asking about my age, my job and my status.
When he spoke, his bushy chest hair, sticking
out between buttons on his boring sweat-soaked
shirt, spoke too. I kept nodding, just to act diplomatic.
But deep down, I apologized on the city's behalf.
It must be hell for a boar like him to grunt
in summer heat. Next, he gave me a short sociology
lecture on gay men in Asia. Tokyo ones are cuter
than Taipei's, who, however, have broader shoulders.
Singaporeans, hot as deep-fried chili crabs. He paused
before he remarked on penises that went up and down
in my city and said he should head home. So I waited
with him for a taxi. The air in those five minutes—
filled with peace after an accidental assault by white
intelligence—was all I loved that night. Finally,
he gave up. He said he would walk a few blocks
to the Sheung Wan Station and catch the last train.
We didn't shake hands or hug. After an empty
farewell, I flew like a yellow-billed egret back to the bar,
crowded with Hong Kong gays, full of attitudes.

FOREIGN EXCHANGE
for Andrea Brittan

"His right nipple smells like his left nipple, which smells like his navel. Every hairless body smells the same in places like Cambodia," the British tourist concludes. There's no season, but one kind of weather here: the sun always copper, casting its colour onto the topless boys whose shoulders are crushed by the shrewd British pounds. Crushed not by armies, but arms of those who suck nothing but the third-world juice with their white lips, dancing tongue and whiter skin. Next year at this time, this boy will see the same daddy, same currency. He will be worshipped as David, but fondled again like a dildo in a cheap hotel bed, in which dignity is dust. With just a soft sudden blow, it disappears like a shadow in darkness. But would he open his eyes? Would he be able to see he's rolled over by a hairy bear born to break bones? All eyes can be blinded by the dollar sign. Back home, the boy will wash his body, soapless and not sobbing, while his daddy will count the stamps in his wrinkled burgundy passport.

DELIVERY

This morning, at the post office, I asked
for stamps that could send a 72.3kg parcel
to the farthest corner from here. The officer,
clueless but professional, took out an atlas
and did some measurements with a ruler.
"That would be Porto Alegre," he said. Having
no idea where it was, I thanked him and left
with a handful of adorable squares that had
the same number of teeth on each side. At home,
I carefully glued each of them on my body,
the cheapest on my feet and the most expensive
on my head. If my body got returned because I
didn't pay enough, I still hoped my head or parts
of my upper body could be delivered safely. Then,
on a note card, I wrote down TO HEAVEN…
I realized my handwriting resembled that of the little
girl I met last night. In my car, she showed me her
school work, which I didn't care. I was more
concerned, as her pa, if she had Down's syndrome,
premenstrual distress and if she had a penis.
"Any of them would bring back luck to your grade,"
I warned, as I did to her friends, like an oracle. So she let
me check to make sure she could be the cream
in class. What an ambitious doll, but too paranoid.
Too worried about the notion of winning, she told
everyone about my alternative tutoring. Just
after daybreak, her mother called me on the world's
behalf, "You've fucked the whole world by fucking
my daughter." I wished to tell her I, like a humble
bee, wanted not the world, but the queen and her
creamy skin. Angry and revengeful vixens were
difficult to deal with, my experience told me.
I decided to give the leviathan under my jackal
pants a rest. I decided, with a bullet and a number
of stamps, I would be carried by dutiful postmen
to another world, where, as I had seen in church
murals, men and girls fluttered in air naked,
unashamed of their charm.

DEAR _____,
After Matthew Yeager

> "... you want friends, you're going to have to write letters to strangers."
> Adrienne Rich

Do you set multiple alarm clocks? After each
one buzzes, do you go back to bed as if the day
had not arrived? Do you stretch your arms?
What about your legs? Do you wash your
face first or brush your teeth? How does your
toothpaste taste? Mint or marshmallow? Bath
or shower? Do you duet with your body
in the running water? And which part sings
in falsetto and which in tenor?
After you dry yourself, does your dog pry
about your nudity? Is he right- or left-pawed?
What flaws does he have? Is he a food
fanatic or a fussy eater? What color is his anus?
Sweetly pink or graphite gray? What about yours?
Do you name him after your father or ex-
lover? Do you keep them anonymous?
Do you keep your toilet seat down? Do you sit
when you piss? How do you roll the toilet paper,
over or under? Who do you think of when you
keep rolling? Do you recycle? Do you steal
the laundry bag and slippers in a hotel room?
Do you sleep naked when you're alone? Do you
avoid rooms at the end of a hallway? Do you
ever touch the Bible in the drawer? What do you
think about Christianity and heterosexuality?
Which one is more helpless? What words do
you always spell wrong? Do you ever have
a typewriter? Or a Polaroid? What is the sexist
sound? Have you ever put your ear next
to a shell and hoped to hear words spoken
by another world? Have you ever smelled your
mother's bras? Did you put them on your head
and play Superman? Are you lactose-intolerant?
Are you HIV positive? Are you positive
about anything? How many phone numbers
of your friends can you remember? How many

of them have slept with you? How do they smell
and moan? Like a swan, a pig or you? Do you look
into a mirror ten times a day? How many
national flags can you recognize? Do you
write an *i* with a little dot or fancy circle? Lasagna
or angel hair? Toothpicks or dental floss? Top or
bottom? Bareback or condom? Are your eyes
blue or brown? Do you highlight your hair?
Are you hairy? What is the highlight of your
day? How was your day before you read this?
Do you look for signs? What book do you have
next to your bed? How tall are you? Where did
you first make out? How old were you? How old
was he? Are you circumcised? Briefs
or boxers? What size? Do you keep a diary?
Do you write about me? Do you wonder
how I look before you sleep?

Nicholas YB Wong

A CORONER'S REPORT ON AN UNKNOWN BODY

You are drunk as a dead fish floating on rum,
on lust and self-pity. So, as you wish, I bring
you home, like a souvenir, and strip you before we
have the courtesy to learn each other's name.

You hair is a satire: skin-thin on both sides, permed
and thick at the top with a few highlights. It still smells
of disco smoke and cheap molding clay, which I
do not need. My hairline is receding, a coastline

getting further away from the land in low tide.
Let me examine your eyes, which, fortunately, are closed.
And yes, they are better shut. When open, they will just
betray you with blankness. Some say the eyes make

an entrance to one's soul. To me, they are a closure
of my fantasies. You are not kind to your ears either.
The right pinna is pierced with a few silvery rings,
It looks like a tambourine. But what sort of youthful

melody does it play? I peep into the auditory canal
to look for your eardrum, where musical notes
are dancing. Then, my finger sails south and finds
your resilient clavicle, which twitches when I caress

along the curve. Wait, a mole, round and black, rests
on your chest plateau. Can I wake you up and tell you
that it is a sign of good fortune? I'd better not. Instead,
I admire the third nipple, as if it were a museum exhibit.

I am not a rapist, so I will leave your briefs untouched.
But through the white translucent cotton, the contour
and density of your crotch sings its own anthem. You are
well-hung, no doubt about it. Your thick thumb and

tall nose have said it all. But you are not that perfect.
The sores on your soles and around your toes
are ossified like fossils. Dry skin flakes off with just
a slight scratch. Too much disco dancing, I bet.

I know they hurt, but my feet are worse, torn after years
of endless cruising and stalking. So I should bestow you
what your body deserves. I will rub your feet gently
and warm them with a pair of new white socks.

Then I will play my favourite Nessun Dorma and climb
over you, with one hand fondling your hairless thighs
and the other stroking my cock, an antique organ
that will sign this report by shooting a few protein drops.

MOTHERS

"There has never been a parent kept alive by a child's love."
- Louise Glück

   1.

The sour breath of May, a bit humid,
climbs onto our bed early in the morning.
It reminds us—Mother's Day, which, in Hong Kong,
is after spring, but not yet summer.

Today is the day when all mothers, dead or living,
join their children. They come out of soil or kitchen
and anticipate delicate dim sum.
They laugh hard at banters that lose meanings on other days.

   2.

Grandma lived as a full human for seventy-six years,
and half a machine for another three.

After she died, a blind psychic yodeled:
grandma'll have four legs

in next life, perhaps a dog. But no worry,
beasts know how to work things out.

In the past, my mom laughed at the blind
who spoke of the present—

I can see with my own eyes, she said.
Now, to her, life is black chaos.

She looks into the eyes of street dogs that tail after her,
wondering if she knows their names.

3.

This morning, grandma looks stout, as she used to,
but her skin glows

after the costly embalming.

She slaves over crispy spring rolls and
the yellow yolk of petit egg tarts.
Her spavined hand reaches out but can only grasp
the chilling air between her fingers.

She cringes. She squints at my mom's carnations,
fathoming why on this maternal day she is excluded—
cold among us and flowerless.

Her body once had a hole, through which she pushed
out my mom, who in turn, pushed out everyone present at the table.

She is hungry—
for food, for our touch, our calling of her name.
She wishes carnations grew
in her world, like weeds and vines that
always sprout around her tombstone.

WIGGERMAN
SCOTT

fantastic accessories

Scott Wiggerman is the author of two books of poetry, *Vegetables and Other Relationships* and *Presence*, forthcoming from Pecan Grove Press. Poems by Wiggerman have been included in *Switched-on Gutenberg*, *Poemeleon*, *Broad River Review*, *Gertrude*, *Boxcar Poetry Review*, and *Southwestern American Literature*, as well as the anthologies *Best Gay Poetry*, *Queer Collection*, and *This New Breed: Gents, Bad Boys, and Barbarians 2*. A frequent workshop instructor, he is also an editor for Dos Gatos Press, publisher of the annual *Texas Poetry Calendar*, now in its fourteenth year. *Wingbeats: Exercises and Practice in Poetry*, a collection Wiggerman is co-editing with his partner, David Meischen, will be released from Dos Gatos Press in 2011.

swig.tripod.com

AT 58, HE DISCOVERS MAKE-UP

Change had been creeping in
like frown lines and crow's feet.
The coupon for free hair coloring—
"let them see who you really are"—
beckoned for weeks
from a refrigerator magnet,
and now this: product to cover
and smooth the creases,
to whisk away years in minutes.

At the video-shoot, a make-up artist
had applied a small regimen
of foundation, concealer, bronzer,
transforming his face for the camera.
After the shoot, he refused
removal of the miraculous emollients,
chose instead to test them
on friends at dinner, to bask
in the lights of a Mexican restaurant
like a dinner theater star.

To preen, he rationalized,
was the right of his species—
and what could be more natural
than a product called Just for Men?

Scott Wiggerman

THE CORAL YUCCA

The coral yucca have awakened, surged
from clumps into the sky—oh, up they rise,
with heads both pink and sure, as though engorged
on privilege. Why try to moralize?
They're only filling nature's role, so up
they soar, extending, fleshing out their long
green stalks, unfettered, proud; each haughty prop
positioned, set to party, join the throng
in orgiastic ecstasy! And yet
already some are spent, declined toward earth
and bent like Dickens' orphans, the regret
of failure on their faces. Can their worth
be this short-lived? How brief this virile term
of upward thrust, how swift the downward squirm.

TO THE BUFF

He glides like a smile across the room,
unaware that I'm awake,
listening to his cast-offs:

the t-shirt that shimmies over his shoulders,
making a slight poof
as it strains free of his head,

the shoes that clump to the floor,
one dull thud after another,
socks that follow like an echo,

the rustle of belt buckle,
a pop and swift zip before trousers
drop like an errant elevator,

the elastic snap of underpants
and the wet-dog shake, a male reflex
to the *carte blanche* of nudity.

I stir as though aroused
from unfinished dreams, quiet
sheets resounding with possibility.

THE WAITER

He's built like a beefcake patty
loaded with all the extras—
extra muscle, extra charm,
deliciously sculpted buns.
He moves away to place our order,
and we hear a sizzle with each step.
We never expected sirloin at Chili's!

When he brings our burgers—
careful, this platter is hot!—
flashing a smile taut as his jeans,
we decide on his gratuity:
a dollar for every meaty inch.
Our appraisals start at seven,
but convincingly escalate to nine:

never underestimate the size
of a hunky waiter's tip.

STILL JANUARY

The cat's been spiraling inward,
her face inseparable from her tail,
a Möbius strip of gray fur.
You've been stratified in sweaters
and sweatshirts, a plush robe
encasing the layers below—
yet you check the thermostat
like a nurse monitors a patient.
At least you move. I haven't
stepped out of the house in two days,
wedged like lost change
among the pillows of the sofa.

Clouds have murked the day
with on-again, off-again drizzle,
the landscape subdued in a trance,
everything wet and forlorn.

All day, I read a novel about 9/11,
glancing out the window
at skies laden in ash,
half-expecting to see bodies
plummet into view,
not seeing so much as a squirrel.
We stay in our homes,
knowing it's no safer here
than anywhere else.

You fidget with your own book,
another cup of green tea,
arms and legs twisted in a huddle
beneath an afghan.
I watch your lips move
with each word
but can't make out a single one.
I think about how the rats in the attic
haven't scratched all weekend.

STAND-OFF

We went to bed like boars, but now
we wake without the strength to fight.
How we lose our passions, and how
the day shades with echoes of night.

Still we brood from hostile corners,
hold on to thoughts of wrong or right
like burnished martyrs, lost mourners—
the day shades with echoes of night.

Lights are dimmed. Love is kept in tow.
We, as polar as black and white,
speak with silence, watch the hours go.
The day shades with echoes of night.

RENOUNCING THE DEVIL

Bare and thick as sin,
his feet smack the forest floor,
rebuff my advances
with each deep slap.
We cannot see the ground
but can taste the darkness,
the lurid shadows
of a confessional.

If he stopped running,
I might lose him,
would never be able to ask,
What are you afraid of?
But all he'd hear is
What are you—?
and that, too, is a question
he won't answer.

BUMP AND SMOOCH

We picked them up while trolling
one of those weekend garage sales.
Yes, they were someone else's trash,
the cheapest kind of costume jewelry:
two imitation-silver seahorse brooches,
each with a tiny rhinestone eye
that even then barely glistened.

Yet we fawned over them
like King Tut's treasures,
shrieking as we pinned them on each other,
shocking the Peoria housewife
who'd never seen two queens in action.

The seahorses became an unspoken pact.
I wore mine to the mall each day
and would squeal with delight
when he'd show up wearing his.
Before we adjusted to sales mode,
we'd gallop to each other like long-lost lovers
and bump our brooches together
amid a flurry of seahorse air-kisses.

Of course, it was the 70's,
and who didn't seem gay?
We had three-inch platform shoes,
low-waisted jeans patched like old tires,
t-shirts tight as blood pressure cuffs,
and hair moussed into helmets.
I wore a ring on every finger,
each as gaudy as a Five-and-Dime counter.
Who was going to notice
an inch-and-a-half brooch
on a collar as wide as a book?

Like seahorses, the times were short-lived.
I kept my tacky little pin,
and somehow I know that he kept his,
our war medals, prized like veterans
buffing silver out of gray.

PLAYING GI JOES

My GI Joe didn't care for camouflage,
that dreary mélange of green and khaki.
He preferred the minimal clothes that I created
with a pair of scissors and poor sewing skills:
hot little loincloths attached with a pin,
paisley ponchos that required only a hole,
a strip of red velvet for a headband or belt.

My GI Joe craved reconnaissance missions.
He would sneak about my sister's room,
raiding Barbie's boutique for fashion ideas,
trying on faux fur and elastic-banded skirts,
tube tops and a white-beaded bridal veil—
forays which seldom produced good fits
but occasionally spawned fantastic accessories.

My GI Joe was a gung-ho exhibitionist.
He'd rip off his Army fatigue jacket,
metal snaps rat-a-tatting like an M-1 rifle;
he'd strut that smooth plastic chest
as if his twelve-inch stature controlled the barracks;
then he'd drop his pants around the ankles,
displaying buttocks as solid as rocks—
an audacious tease for one without a penis.

My GI Joe learned to take a lot of pain.
He'd volunteer to cross into enemy terrain,
where he'd be captured without a struggle,
stripped like a go-go boy, and thrown into a cell.
Tied up, disciplined, tortured into a frenzy,
he was a master of man-to-man endurance,
revealing only name, rank, and serial number
as a sly grin edged toward the scar on his cheek,
a mark that covered so many of our secrets.

DANIELS
CARL MILLER

jamie bell, I hope you're flattered

Carl Miller Daniels lives in ruggedly masculine Homerun, Virginia. Over the years, his poems have appeared in lots of nice places: *Chiron Review*; *CommonLine E-Journal*; *FUCK!*; *My Favorite Bullet*; *Thieves Jargon*; *Underground Voices*; *Rusty Truck*; *Wormwood Review*; *Zen Baby*; *Zygote in my Coffee*; and *5AM*, to name a few. Daniels has had three chapbooks published in the past dozen years or so: *Riot Act* and *Shy Boys at Home* (both published by Chiron Review Press)—and *Museum Quality Orgasm* (published by Future Tense Books). On three separate occasions, Daniels has been nominated for Pushcart Prizes. He and his lover, Jon (aka "the sweetest man in the world"), have lived together for over 30 years.

POE, HAWTHORNE, AND MELVILLE—SIR!

a sunny spot in the middle of
the woods: there's a stream nearby.
it's making honest-to-gosh babbling sounds
as the sexy naked big-dicked ROTC cadet and
the sexy naked big-dicked american lit major
sit talking to each other.
"here, have some more weed," says
the sexy naked big-dicked ROTC cadet as he
passes the joint over to the
sexy naked big-dicked american lit major.
the sexy naked big-dicked american lit major inhales
deeply. "i'd like to suck you off now," he says.
one thing quickly leads to another,
and, very soon,
each of them freshly sucked off by the other, they
lie there side by side, still naked,
looking up into the big blue sky.
"your cum tastes like old books,"
the sexy naked big-dicked ROTC cadet says to the
sexy naked big-dicked american lit major.
"well, your cum tastes like gunpowder,"
the sexy naked big-dicked american lit major says
to the sexy naked big-dicked ROTC cadet.
"since when have your ever eaten an old book?" says
the sexy naked big-dicked american lit major.
"and since when have you ever eaten gunpowder?"
says the sexy naked big-dicked ROTC cadet.
a moment of silence ensues.
"i guess this means we're in love,
doesn't it?" says the sexy naked big-dicked
american lit major.
"that we are," says the sexy naked big-dicked ROTC cadet.
"good," says the sexy naked big-dicked
american lit major.
"real good," says the sexy naked big-dicked
ROTC cadet. when the sun starts to set,
they embrace each other, and
hang on tight, lilac and vinegar,
oil and water, hot like
moon-lit steam.

TENDON

"me me me me i'm just
so me-centered. when will
it ever stop? when will
i ever really care
about anyone or
anything else?" thinks
the sexy record-breaking
collegiate swimmer,
as he stands up from
the toilet, flushes it,
and adjusts his speedo
to perfect ball-hugging
cock-defining fit,
and off he strides
toward the pool
and satisfaction
and victory, the flex of his
own muscles the glide
of his own skin through
the blue-tinted
chlorinated water
will leave him
giddy almost sick
with joy, high
as a white fluffy cloud,
serious masturbation
to follow soon
thereafter, and then, as usual,
when he's spurting cum
he'll be thinking about
the possibility of
finding his long-lost twin,
a constant fixation of
his: the find, the two of them,
him and his identical twin,
together: it wouldn't
really be incest,
not really, DNA being
what it is, and
flesh moody as a dream.

VERGIL DIED 19 B.C. - AND SCOTT'S PECS

the truth is,
the sexy naked big-dicked teenage boy
has the hots for scott, president
of the high-school latin club. scott is
a bodybuilder. scott has
won teenage bodybuilding competitions
locally and nationally.
scott is a high-school senior.
the sexy naked big-dicked teenage boy
is a high-school junior, and he
has the hots for scott.
his
having the hots for scott is
a secret, though.
truth is,
it's quite doubtful that scott is gay,
and
the sexy naked big-dicked teenage boy
doesn't admit that he, himself, is gay.
but there sits
the sexy naked big-dicked teenage boy,
alone on his bed, his latin iii textbook open
on his desk, his
vergil assignment
awaiting translation,
his big thick dick hard and throbbing,
and he's thinking about
vergil, and latin,
but mostly he's thinking
about
scott.
soon, the sexy naked big-dicked teenage boy
just lies back on his bed and starts
jerking off: for a few blissful
moments, his mind seems clear,
precisely focused, on the
wonderful feeling that his own
highly stimulated great big hard dick
is giving to him.
as he spurts cum, he pictures

scott's broad sexy bodybuilder shoulders,
the open page of that latin iii textbook,
and vergil's voice sloshes
around inside his head
like doom gone wild,
death a certainty,
where is vergil's body today
anyway? probably just
dust now, and
the sexy naked big-dicked teenage boy,
his chest and belly drenched in his
own cum, rotates the image
of scott clockwise, counterclockwise,
and the years spin by like
latin—everyone spoke it
back then—even
while getting fucked.

SPRINGSUMMER WINTERFALL

the sexy naked sophomore college boy and the
scrawny skinny naked freshman college boy
are sitting in their dorm room on
the bottom bunk, legs crossed, facing each other.
they are eating crackers.
the scrawny skinny naked freshman college boy
has sprouted quite a nice big hardon, and
the sexy naked sophomore college boy
comments: "you've got a hardon."
the scrawny skinny naked freshman college boy
replies: "these are certainly excellent crackers,
aren't they?"
then, with almost the accompanying "SPROING!" sound,
the sexy naked sophomore college boy sprouts
a nice big hardon, too.
the two boys sit there eating their crackers
and staring at each other's hardons.
"JERK-OFF BREAK!!" they both shout in
perfect unison.
and that's exactly what they do,
the sexy naked sophomore college boy and the
scrawny skinny naked freshman college boy,
sitting there across from each other
on the bottom bunk, jerking themselves off
until they spurt cum all over their own
naked chests and bellies.
then, with one graceful, seemingly pre-rehearsed
motion, they each grab a handful of tissues
from the nearby tissue box, and wipe
themselves off.
"well," says
the sexy naked sophomore college boy to the
scrawny skinny naked freshman college boy,
"back to the crackers?"
"they are tasty, aren't they?" says
the scrawny skinny naked freshman college boy,
"and salty, too."
"we like salt," say the two boys together.
"we do we do we do."

SPREAD 'EM

again, the exalted one has declared himself to
be the absolute best, and, once
again, no one is disputing.
of course,
the exalted one is hot-looking, sexy,
physically stunning, and big-dicked. also,
he has a great face, with a wonderful smile.
he has a great personality, too.
not a mean bone in his body. people always
love him when they meet him. and those that
get to have sex with him, always
enjoy the experience. everybody always cums.
with a smile on their face, and
an ecstatic pleasurable moan.
if only the exalted one wouldn't
persist in referring to himself
in that manner, though. yes,
he really does refer to himself
as "the exalted one." it's
kind of off-putting. it would,
in fact, be downright annoying,
if it weren't so goddamn true.

DEGREE

out of the slurry of the coal fire, strides
the hottest boy you could ever imagine.
he looks to be about 18 years old,
but who knows? maybe he's really 500 years old,
or 5000 years old. who can tell?
but he strode right out of that fire,
naked, sexy-looking as all get-out,
hair on fire, his eyes shy,
and yet eager, too.
try to touch him, though,
and your hand gets
burned. try to kiss him,
and you'll pull back
before you feel the sizzle.
he's naked all the time.
no need to try to put clothes
on him, though, they'd just catch
fire and burn off anyway.
he likes to sit in the
local coffee shop, and,
if anybody's coffee
gets cold, he just
grabs ahold of the cup
for a couple seconds, and
that heats it right back up.
he seems to appreciate
the "thank-you's" that
he receives. they seem
heart-felt, and genuine.
he likes that, being
appreciated for something
he can do rather than
for what he looks like, as
he sits at the corner
booth, the one with
the metal chairs,
their sharp little
feet melting the
wax on the
cold slick floor.

WRESTLING WITH CHANGE

when the percolator malfunctioned, coffee
went all over the kitchen:
the walls, the countertops, the floor.
well, the two sexy young men
had been in the bedroom
having sex during the percolator malfunction.
when they walked naked and
sweaty into the kitchen and saw the
mess, one of the two sexy naked young men
said "FUCK!" and the other of
the two sexy naked young men
said "GODDAMNIT TO GODDAMN HELL!"

**

clean-up took a long time,
and, during the process,
the two sexy young men
threw the old-fashioned
percolator out into the back yard,
and left it lying there,
like a little gray corpse.

**

then they went out and bought
a brand-new drip-style coffee maker.
they had liked that old-fashioned
percolator, though. it made
good, rich, old-fashioned coffee.
the new drip-style coffee maker
wasn't bad, though, they
had to admit, that evening.
they stood there in the kitchen,
and stared at the new gadget.
"it does look pretty good,

doesn't it?" said one
of the two young men.
"yeah, kind of like a space-age
rocket launcher doesn't it?" said
the other young man.

**

then they went into the den,
watched an old movie on tv,
and, when there was a part
in the movie where an
old-fashioned coffee percolator
was making coffee,
the two young men smiled
wistfully.
"damn percolator," said one of
the two young men.
"but i do kinda feel sorry for
it," said
the other young man,
"lying out in the back yard like that,
all cold and alone."

**

in the morning
they gave it a decent burial,
near a rose bush,
a red one, with
especially big thorns.

SHOPPING LIST, FOLDED IN THE MIDDLE

time standing like a dinosaur
poised to pounce,
as the sexy big-dicked country boy
sucked on mark's big schlongy
hard pumping dick.
the sexy big-dicked country boy
and
his cousin mark
only did this the one time,
and then it was over,
a thing of the past,
never talked about ever
ever again between them,
or to anyone else,
as far
as
the sexy big-dicked country boy
knew.
now,
the wind moving the willow leaves
and their long feral branches,
the sexy big-dicked country boy
is a man, with wrinkles
on his face,
and memories inside
his warm moist brain
that skitter and spark from
brain-ridge to
brain-ridge, and
fire like pistons, as
if still having the
very best time of their
little wet pink lives.

yes Yes YES

in the microseconds before
the sexy athletic big-dicked teenage boy
is getting ready to spurt cum,
his eyes flash like fire,
or they shut tight,
or he squints as if he's in pain.
yes, in the microseconds right before
the sexy athletic big-dicked teenage boy
spurts cum, he may look as though he's in pain,
but he's not.
he's in the throes of so much
pleasure that
the honesty in his eyes
is of confusion—how can there
be this much pleasure in life?
how can there be this much
pleasure on earth?
how can there be this much
pleasure going on at the
tip of my dick?
and then,
the sexy athletic big-dicked teenage boy
spurts out big hot gooey dollops of
cum,
splats them up against the wall
of the shower stall in
which he is jerking off,
and he's suddenly so
sure of the
goodness of life,
so sure of
the goodness of spurting
cum,
so sure of
the goodness of being
a sexy athletic big-dicked teenage boy,
that, he,
just for a moment,
he's sure of everything else,
too.

INDULGENCE IS THE SINCEREST FORM OF SAYING YES

Jamie Bell (star of BILLY ELLIOT and THE CHUMSCRUBBER
and MISTER FOE), are you secretly reading my poetry?
Jamie Bell, you beautiful big-dicked young man, are
you secretly reading my poetry
about beautiful big-dicked young men,
beautiful big-dicked young men just like you?

Jamie Bell, i hope you're flattered, and
not creeped out, that i can so easily
picture you totally naked, lying on
your back atop your bed, and you
are so gently oh you are
so gently tugging on your big
hard smooth dick. when you spurt
cum, your eyes flash like
mystical sparks and your
sweet charming crooked little grin peeks
through your wet tongue-licked
lips.

Jamie Bell, are you secretly
reading my poetry about
beautiful big-dicked young men
who do the sort of things
that i imagine you do,
in the privacy of your
own room, on your bed,
alone, experiencing
the joy you experience
at touching your beautiful
body in the respectful
and reverent ways that
you touch your nipples,
and dick, and balls,
and let your fingers
linger over just the
tips of your untrimmed
pubic hair.
you are

a wild man, there
all alone, thrashing
about, dreaming of
my sweet
sexy poems,
and me.

ONCE AGAIN, AUTUMN ARRIVES

the sexy naked big-dicked teenage boy stood
around squirting raw grapes into his mouth.
it had been a good harvest, and the
grapes this year were especially sweet.
he squirted one grape after another into
his mouth, and he swallowed everything that
went into his mouth, seeds and all.
he flung all the eviscerated
grape skins onto the ground,
and there were soon a lot of them,
wet droopy purple husks,
all around his sexy naked feet.

his step-brother came out of the house
and told him to stop eating grapes,
and to put on some clothes, for a change.
he didn't really mean it, though.

the step-brother was hunky and
sexy and often wore nothing himself.

they had a unique relationship.
not exactly incest, but
something kinda close to it.

the sexy naked big-dicked teenage boy
and his hunky step-brother often
watched pornographic movies together,
while jerking themselves off,
but they thought that that didn't really count.

they are probably right.
still, though,
it's only natural to wonder...

on full-moon nights when
the wolves are howling
outside their window, they
sometimes sleep together.
for comfort and warmth.

NO EXCUSES

i'm 58 years old now, and
i remember the days when i was
in college and lived in the dorm
and the main criteria for a friend
seemed to be he was sexy and he
made me laugh. and we
talked all the time. about
everything. some nights,
standing there in the big
dorm showerroom on my hall,
talking naked to each other,
about anything, everything,
grades, mold, food, eyes move
up and down each other's
bodies, nothing
sexual going on, and yet,
everything sexual
going on.

BODHRÁN
AHIMSA TIMOTEO
his lips full of medicine

Ahimsa Timoteo Bodhrán is the author of *Antes y después del Bronx: Lenapehoking*, winner of the New American Press Chapbook Contest; and the editor of an international queer Indigenous issue of *Yellow Medicine Review: A Journal of Indigenous Literature, Art, and Thought*. His work appears in over a hundred publications in Africa, the Américas, Asia, Australia, Europe, and the Pacific. He received his M.F.A. in Creative Writing from Brooklyn College and is currently an American Studies Ph.D. candidate at Michigan State University. The author of a new chapbook, *South Bronx Breathing Lessons*, he is completing *Yerbabuena/Mala yerba*, *All My Roots Need Rain: mixed-blood poetry & prose* and *Heart of the Nation: Indigenous Womanisms, Queer People of Color, and Native Sovereignties*. Of the poems printed here, "How to Make Love to a Dying Rican" and "Nueva York/Lenapehoking" appeared in *Yellow Medicine Review: A Journal of Indigenous Literature, Art, and Thought*; "Post" appeared in *Blue Mesa Review*; "powder" appeared in *Eleven Eleven*; "Procession" appeared in *Faultline*; and "Vergüenza" appeared in *Carousel*.

www.msu.edu/~bodhran

HOW TO MAKE LOVE TO A DYING RICAN

1. Remember he is still living.

2. Remember you, too, will die.

3. Try not to rush either.

4. Kiss his lips full of medicine.
   Rub his back full of knots.

5. Remember he wants you alive;
   don't be foolish.

6. Realize you will both become
   statistics.

7. Remember the way his face looked
   in the movie he made. Remember
   it in the one you are now making.

8. Tell him he can play any role.

9. Inscribe in memory
   the sound of his voice, feel of
   his hands on your chest, waist,
   hips. The trace of his finger across your
   lips, yours in the recess
   of his ass.

10. Keep rum and candy
    nearby. They keep the gods happy.

11. Tell him you will visit
    in the next life, and this island
    will again be filled
    with trees.

12. In the canoe of our own
    making, we travel upstream.
    Fill the hollow of his hull.
    Husk the corn from his frame.

13. Cacique dance.

    Bless his limbs with flight.

PROCESSION

I do not know how old I am.

I am at the gun range, trying to avoid splinters in my seat. The men (my mother included) wear headphones to block out the sound. It's been a few minutes since I've touched a gun. I know not to touch the shells; too hot, they'll burn your fingers. Wait a few seconds, then they'll be warm. And try to find the shiny ones amidst the dirt and sand. I imitate ants, hulls building hills, the release of Pixy Stix into a throat.

Summer is a good soda, and sweat, and paper turning to ash. Reliefs disintegrate before my eyes as I tongue the hole of Life Savers.

The metal tip is soft and gray; like lead, it is soft and greasy on paper.

On the hill, discus fly into air, Europeans aim at clay. Here in the valley, we use what Father has brought from work. Soon, only the edges of skin are visible. This is a sign of a good shot, good shooting experience. Even though free, we try not to waste paper. Sometimes, the weight of a page tears on its own.

I am here with family. I am drawing or perhaps writing.
I am taking a break from the proceedings.

POWDER

1.
bullethole in stomach, bullethole through chest. powder taken with meals, to digest properly, this experience. veggie soul food, cramps, the anglofication of your name. *Who wants to be a target anymore?* colored contacts, in-acuvue. drive-bys in téjas, cali. triangulate this one. my brother, knife through fibers of leg, bullet through flesh of arm, other brother holding the gun. later cop, later security guard, later photographer. we are all siblings, know each other, trim trio, triage, claim each other as kin through the damage we do. *I fucked you up pretty badly, didn't I? Let me see the scar.* pride in patchwork, # of nails; paper clip the wound. teflon stomach. you pressing against me in hallway, above mission rooftop, refusing my mouth. a slow, easy pressure on my shoulders, easing me down. you won't kiss me, but expect me to go down on you in a dirty hallway without a condom while our sisters, blood not chosen, chosen not blood, wait downstairs. hours on the hand of a minute clock, that small, ticking, pacemaker of your heart. *Always waitin on a man, always waitin on some mutherfuckin man.* to make out with you is sexist. yellow resin, everywhere, mandatory, replacing powder, enlarged nasal capacity, disintegrated cartilage, shark fin soup, old wood glue, Sunday sum. De La Vega's tapemarks on the street. pages of a book gone bad. residue of termites. outline of this love.

2.
want to kiss your scar, lay lips there against puckered skin, an unknown, knowable fleshiness. how sensitive you are.

3.
Sitting on your bed, something tears in me, comes undone. *feel as if i'm gonna die. want hospital, feel punished. something wrong.* I am afraid my stitches have broken, that I am bleeding inside, internal, that our roughhousing on your roof, ruptured something, hernia surgery eight months ago. You ignore me as I keel over, bend over, two sisters coming to my aid. They are there for me. You are not. Eventually, the pain subsides. *stop crying.* Still frightened, promise to check myself in the morning and the next couple of days. Probably just some scar tissue breaking. The doctor told me this would happen. You break something free in me. I let you go.

POST

This is sobering. The years I woke up in different cities, no memory of means of transport, others carrying me into bed. The time I drank three liters of wine in one night, and was fine, stumbling on beaches outside Venice at 17, waking up buzzed, still having eyebrows, drinking more at lunch, later, in what is to become post-Czechoslovakia. Oktoberfest in Mai, post-Mauer. It's amazing what a scholarship can do. The time I kicked a Black girl in the stomach when they tried to take me home, out of the frat house, the fights I got into, bruises I left, punches I threw (away). The boy I stalked and would not leave alone. Also 17. How she never answered my letters. How the school I was visiting put me on wait list, later accepted me (but not financially). How crazy and near the edge I was that year. Señor senior of la escuela. I'm amazed I've graduated from anyplace. Jamesway Higher School of Learning. The closet will do that to you. Class closet. Race closet. The white couple I told I needed to be in abusive relationships with because I felt worthless after being raped. Of course, I never used those words: *rape. abuse. worth.* Amazing how any language fits inside our mouths. How they all said he was such a nice guy. *Look at the flowers he b(r)ought you.* "I need pain so that I'll recognize pleasure." My father worked hard. I never saw him. What we use for education; entry level 101/701 course. Remedial, -mediation. c(c). Do not collect 200 (milliliters). What we send on to others. Go back to go. Lose all property, hotels, friends. Open this gift. It is mine(d). The brown boy on crystal I wasted a year and a half with. The way I tried to walk out of third story windows. How I do not remember a good portion of my youth. Brownouts. Fellowship. Shrapneled skin. Falling off a bike. Other means of income. The hatred I have for alcoholics, anyone with slurred speech, missed step, teeth on concrete, stumbling. The way I refuse people the dollar. Why we all need dentists. Their empty cup. The way I flushed my mother's cigarettes down the garbage, threw them in the toilet. Bailey's und Rotwein and Eierlikör were my favorites. How superior I felt each time I saw someone else vomit or have hangover, fall flat-face into the ground. *Fuckin drunks.* I made it without programs, the. The way each of my brothers has become my father, and some man (n)one of us have met. Needing burial, dirt. I wonder how many different drug combinations between us. My education: "Here is someone who drank and drived/drove." Scalp in a windshield. Body flung far. Polaroid Kodak moment. An aunt in jail. Just say no. "Use your seatbelt. Wear it." Making fun of neighbors who go to AA and Alateen meetings. Us shooting the dog. My mother offering the father a beer, despite the wife's protests. *He was a good man.* How good was he? Brother MP-ed into detox. Buckling up.

We never fucked. But I still hear your voice in my ear as if you were pulling out of me and reminding me to breathe, our back-chest, swamp. I know at this meeting, someone is supposed to make the coffee, but I never learned how. Drainage. Filtration.

The way I drank it as a child—Strawberry Quik.

>Which substance, instant instance?
>What it means to do without you.

This tree steals water from the other ones. It doesn't belong here. It is very thirsty. But koalas like it. See how they teleport on TV?

Why we took a photo before it. Some way of remembering. Mangrove. A/TSI solidarity.

Is there some other way to do service? Stay sober?

We think we'll make it around the lake in time.

My letters keep on getting returned. You never sent me your new address.

The sun is setting. Someone is waiting.

Drink.

VERGÜENZA

He didn't realize the shame of being Native was the same as the shame in being queer. The shame of wanting to touch something, someone, his hands reaching towards trees but looking around before touching, or touching so brief it might be brusk, might bruise the branches, tear a leaf, rip acorn from what was once tender grasp. Soon he wondered the ways in which, during the years he has closeted, was his touch sometimes quick, veering to be discovered, and still now, out with it all, was he wondering, wondering with that, wondering in what further ways he refrained, wanted to, refrained again, from touching the limbs of men, their warm trunks, their strong bodies, and did he turn from them the way he turned from trees, unfortunate, into the night?

NUEVA YORK/LENAPEHOKING

Cañón

Sometimes she looks up through her tenement window at the projects across the way, their red brick against blue sky, and she thinks she is home. Mesas cut and beveled against turquoise. The street, a dry arroyo. Riverbed-quiet in the early morning. One day walking home, she swore she saw corn, over a story high. A girl could reach out her window and eat it. Cigarillos, they call them. Shaped by man, true, but still, these stones, they never left her.

north night sky

Grandfather, each night
you created; arrows
to increasing light;
to anchor me here,

I look up at the work
guiding my eye
I use it
this bedrock born
before these buildings.

history

The original purpose of the Bronx Zoo was to house animals.

Riverdale

How many of us
died here ; how many still
in the service of whites?

Abuela

Hunts Point, Mott Haven,
and Soundview are not just the
homes of dead rappers.

possibility/maxim

If you can find beauty
in the way spit freezes,

you can survive
this city.

common (or myth of the calles)

only diamonds
can cut
diamonds. your con-
crete shapes me from coal.

why i wanted skywalker for a confirmation name

Kanien´keha heard high
    up in the skyscrapers
        language hovering above
            us
        ancestors drifting down
    abuelo en el cielo
shimmering night sky

human history II

Angels tell us: Ellis was not the only island.

"Ain't no In-di-

-ans in NYC"

I go to speak
but only half
        m-
            -y mouth
                is there.

WILLMAN
CHUCK

dreaming of conception

Chuck Willman is a self-taught writer with an Associate of General Studies Degree from Indiana University (which took 13 years to complete due, in part, to his child-like attention span). He's had several erotic stories published under the pseudonym Ethan Cox, as well as a couple poems a few years ago (including "Pussy," which appeared in *Christopher Street*). A long-term PWA, he lives in Las Vegas with his partner of 23 years, Gerry Snyder, a high school counselor, and their beloved dog, Buddy. Somewhat delusional, Chuck believes he's a descendant of Pan, and romps naked in the desert, and other places, whenever possible. He is also eternally grateful to Bryan Borland for his support, kindness, and generosity, and for re-awakening the desire to write and submit work.

panzpoet@gmail.com

A SHIFT IN THE CURRENT

Fifty-five minutes from the first call to their arrival.
I called 911 two more times,
asking if the delay was because
I said it was my *partner* who needed help.
Pacing from front door to bedroom,
terrified, angry, afraid, frustrated,
preparing for the crash.
My sister on my cell phone
telling me to breathe.
I shoved our new puppy in the spare bathroom
when the fire truck, ambulance, and police car
pulled up, their sirens stinging the silent night air,
spinning lights against the black October sky
making it look like there was a block party.

A uniformed army bounced up the stairs
with enough emergency equipment
to rescue the neighborhood.
While four paramedics tended to you,
I was interrogated by the team of male guerrilla cops,
chests puffed as if my scrawny frame was a threat,
or their manhood was challenged studying
the nude male artwork all over our walls,
asking if we had "problems" or had fought—
did I have reason to *kill you!*

I wasn't allowed near you, motionless on the bed
as the cops examined a drinking glass for signs of
sediment on the floor next to our queen-sized bed,
or other evidence of foul play, they said.

I was making dinner when you came out pale and shaking.
I swallowed something—call for help, you said.

In an instant everything changed.

After eighteen years what pulled this trigger?
We'd gone through everything together,
even if just to spite those who said

we'd never make it.
My sister prepared me:
medicines in plastic bags so they can see them,
another bag with loose-fitting clothes
for your stay—you might be there a while—
NO strings. NO belts. NO shoelaces.
Her experience came in handy.

You swallowing a hefty handful
of Clonazepam tablets,
with another of Tylenol PM
was serious trouble.

Neighbors stood on their porches
as you were loaded up.
I was told to follow,
then sat waiting, wondering, worrying—
waving our notarized Power of Attorney paperwork
to convince the Gestapo staff I needed to be there.

At *midnight* I'm allowed in—
told you'd be transferred to a psychiatric hospital
first thing in the morning for your 72-hour
"mandatory observation," like a monkey or a rat.
You were sound asleep behind the curtain,
lifeless, chalk-white, ankles and wrists strapped to the bed.
(A fantasy of yours, but this wasn't a fantasy or game.)
I.V.s jammed into both arms.
Machines everywhere making awful noises
like annoying toys on Christmas morning.
A male nurse with the bedside manner of an SS guard says,
"We pumped his stomach. It took a while.
The motherfucker came pretty close to succeeding."
I stroked your forehead, wanting to sneak you out,
and asked why you had to be tied down.
"We don't know when he'll wake,
or what he'll try when he does."

I was told to leave. I'd be called when you were moved.
Even though I quit smoking a year earlier,
I raced into the first open gas station
for two packs of Camels,

chain-smoking on the phone with my sister.
I cleaned up and cradled
our poor, little Chihuahua, Buddy,
after he shit all over the bathroom and himself,
then scrubbed the grease stain on our carpet
left by the paramedics' gurney,
feeling guilty that I was glad I didn't have to
clean up any blood.
But you could never stand the sight of it.
Cutting yourself would never be an option.

I slept for two hours on the sofa
with Buddy curled on top of my chest.

In the morning I called your family,
telling them you didn't want to
speak to them, yet.
"How could I *not* have seen this coming?"
"Why didn't I prevent it?"
I stayed off the phone for the rest of the day.

When I got to your new hospital
I waited again before being led in
with other family members,
a herd of us silent and numb,
led through a series of doors,
locked in front and behind us,
down long corridors like a prison,
or the Starship Enterprise.

Patients were sent to the Day Room
with thick, wire-reinforced windows,
bizarre "crafts" displayed on walls
from earlier "guests"
like an elementary Homeroom.
There were tables and chairs in clusters
no one dared to move.

There you were, alone,
exhausted, ashamed, sad,
sorry.

We faced each other as if for the first time—
shy, guarded, unsure of what to say.
You laughed at my Homeroom analogy,
and I knew we'd be okay.

You did your time.
A loud cry for help,
as they say.
Finally you had a label—
a diagnosis: *bipolar disorder.*

Like me.
Yours would be treated, too.

We found ourselves tossed into the same boat
with a wicked storm swirling around us,
once again determined to weather it together,
to spite everyone who said we'd never make it.

PUSSY

"Hey, Pussy! I'm talking to you!"
I guess I was being included,
but I couldn't answer cuz
my heart was pounding so hard
and my mouth wouldn't move.
My mouth couldn't move.
So they knew I was just a Pussy
cuz I never said anything, and
took the jabs and shoves,
and froze as their laughter roared.
The laughter roared.
And I'd grit my teeth
to not lose a tear,
cuz I couldn't let 'em see
I was afraid,
or how much it hurt.
How much it hurt.
And when they'd finally walk away,
feeling strong and right,
with that conquering grin
as their final say,
I'd stand,
still gritting my teeth,
locked in place,
no trace of a tear yet,
proving I could do it;
I could be strong
and not be a Pussy.
But then I'd breathe,
and my body would untie
itself on the knots,
and I'd sniffle and blink.
Maybe I could at least
not wail in agony and humiliation
here or now.
Not this time,
cuz I couldn't help it.
And they'd watch me sob and shake,
walking home alone,

where I'd lock myself in.
Locked away.
No one can see.
Not even me.
And I'd dread
walking the next day,
cuz I knew it'd just happen again,
"Hey, Pussy! I'm talking to you,"
still.

HAVING YOUR BABY

We had only "done it"
once,
but I knew that's all it took
to take.
The first time was the sweetest
invasion,
and we were both more than willing
to try.

Two teen
boys
pretending we were only
experimenting,
swearing like blood brothers to keep
our secret.

I was hopelessly in love
with you,
while all you wanted was a
receptacle,
a warm, *real* place to
practice
so you'd be prepared for another's
real thing.

I didn't care, eager to let you
inside,
desperate to feel like I
mattered.

When it was all over you
grinned,
then got up and dressed to play
basketball
with the other neighborhood
boys.

I, however, laid there dreaming of
conception,

knowing a part of you remained
inside me,
padding the front of my
underwear
with wads of toilet paper—
your baby—
that I was going to carry to
full term
without making you feel
responsible.

Under my shirt, the toilet paper wads
grew
secretly as days turned into
weeks
until I almost got caught
in gym,
and I found out about
miscarriage.

I still allowed you to
"practice"
with me anytime you had the
urge,
but I decided I was too young to
be pregnant,
and pretended to go on the
pill.

DESERT

It is quiet and still, now that the earth rests.
Yawning canyons exhale the sweet smell of sagebrush.

Untouched hills display the vivid jewels of flowering cactus
Behind gorges split open over more time than anyone can fathom.

Serrated edges of cliffs, and walls of carved boulders stand guard, while
Mountains of sandstone and clay stained vermillion, gold, and purple

Scratch the belly of a turquoise sky.
The air is warm and soothing, gentle as a lover's whisper.

Untamed desert, holding the secrets of a million yesterdays, where
Only the raw truth of an angry earth exists, and fossils still live.

I feel at home here—it's where I go to escape, with my own secrets,
To be naked in the sun, completely alone, for hours at a time, roaming

Intentionally unnoticed, somehow part of this wild, desolate landscape;
Weathered, close to extinction—diseased, but forgiven and free here.

I'm a contaminated carcass rotting above ground, an optical illusion
Picked clean, crumbling, cracking, and crackling inside like a bonfire;

A skeleton glowing like an X-ray, translucent skin stretched like thin
leather over bones brittle as kindling, like a thousand year old drum.

I have the belly of a starving child; and spindly, fragile limbs.
My hypnotic azure eyes, once a beacon holding strangers hostage

So I'd never sleep alone, now dull and sunken; long, blond mane
That whipped wildly like a field of wheat in a storm, gone.

Throughout what is left of my body, I hear and feel the snapping
As white-hot blood creeps through charred veins like lava,

Then cruelly freezes back into ancient glaciers without warning.
The pain is excruciating, unbearable, constant.

For twenty-two years I've counted T-cells.
Counted the buckets of tainted blood drained from scorched veins.

Counted and consumed handfuls of prescribed poison.
Counted on their endless lists of crippling side effects.

Counted trips to doctors and clinics and hospitals.
Counted birthdays, as each one is a surprise.

I'm only one of the wounded, the dying, adrift in a rancid bloody sea.
There are too many bodies tired of fighting for anyone to rescue.

This virus turned me into a corpse lurking among the living
Like a shadow—invisible, unheard, ignored, forgotten.

I'd crawl through fire today to be wanted again—
Desired, craved, consumed, bartered for—touched.

Each day I wait for my stay of execution, or the hour
I'll be taken, knowing the odds and history are not in my favor.

I'll answer the desert's howl, as long as my scrawny legs carry me;
To feel its life and be rejuvenated—with any luck, becoming a fossil.

THE LESSON

I don't know where I got the balls.

I caught the seductive stare of a six foot husky man near thirty,
wearing dirty jeans and an Army jacket on a balmy summer night
at the 7-11where I occasionally stole a copy of *The Advocate* newspaper,
tucking it in the back of my jeans, racing home to masturbate
gazing at the grainy black and white pictures of naked men,

or men in jock straps in the ads in back, yearning for a man I could touch. I bought Marlboro Reds with a forged note the pimple-faced clerk never read. After the man bought his tall can of Old Milwaukee and pack of Kools, he left the store, and I followed him down the narrow alley, my heart pounding in my ears when he turned around, exhaling a cloud of smoke, my dick half-hard.

I caught up with him near a street light glowing at the edge of the unlit high school football field down the street from my house where he had stopped, taking swigs from the can tightly wrapped in a brown paper bag. I asked him for a light. We stood next to each other in silence.
So what are you up to, he finally asked with a slight sneer.

He unbuttoned his Army jacket exposing a bare, hairy, barrel chest and fuzzy belly. I watched his huge Adam's apple bob as he took a big gulp of the beer. *Hanging out,* I said. He handed the can to me. I took a couple sips, trying not to shake. We were quiet again, and then he stomped out his Kool with his boot. *I'll see ya,* he said. As he walked away, I took a quick drag from my cigarette, exhaled and blurted out as fast as I could: *I want to blow you.*

He turned, lips curling into a roguish grin seeing the excitement flash in my eyes. He took another long swig from his can without saying anything, moving to a cluster of dark bushes at the field's edge, and unzipping his jeans. I dropped my cigarette and walked toward him, and he clutched me in his big paws.

With the smell and taste of beer and tobacco on his breath he kissed me, his big, moist lips warm as fresh baked bread with butter melting over my mouth. Saliva ran down our chins as if sharing a ripe peach. Jeans were shoved to our ankles, releasing hot erections poking into the darkness like branding irons.

He electrocuted me, nibbling and grazing my neck with his scruffy, dark beard before peeling my T-shirt over my head. He took the Army jacket off, opening it over the ground, guiding our aroused bodies down and spreading me like a buffet before opening his legs to smother my face with his big, hairy genitals. The aroma of sweat made my mouth water for its first taste of a man's penis. I eagerly let him fill my mouth with his plump cock, sniffing his thick black bush.

He nuzzled and swallowed my aching dick, and it was better than I ever imagined. His salty skin, sticky pre-come, and my saliva created a frothy mix in my mouth, and I opened wider, feeling his entire length deep into my throat, making me gag. But I didn't stop, inhaling and savoring the moist pubic hair that tickled my nose. We gorged like cannibals, sloppy grunts leaking from our assiduous mouths

before he turned to slide his furry trunk against my hairless stomach, wet cocks colliding until we shuttered—our naked torsos sweat-soaked and semen-soldered. He cradled me the way lovers do before wiping our bellies with his sleeve. We stood to dress, and he took my giddy face in his calloused hands, kissing me softly before walking slowly back into the dark night like an illusion.

I stumbled home through the empty field, exhilarated by his scent smeared all over my face, hands, stomach—proof of a secret stain I didn't want to remove. I ran upstairs to shower, unable to calm my erection under the cool spray. For the next week I searched that field every night. I loitered around the 7-11, waited by *our* bushes, praying I'd find the phantom lover I never saw again.

I was twelve.

BORLAND BRYAN

southern boys like us

Bryan Borland is the editor of *Assaracus*. Coaxed into self-publishing by the late John Stahle, Borland's first book, *My Life as Adam* (Sibling Rivalry Press), was one of only five collections of poetry included on the American Library Association's "Over the Rainbow" list of notable LGBT-focused work published in 2010. The response to *Adam* and Stahle's passing led Borland to create *Assaracus* in January of 2011. He dedicates this selection of poems to the recently-deceased Vytautas Pliura, whose poem "Thomas" changed his life.

www.bryanborland.com

AN OUTSIDER'S GUIDE TO GAY MARRIAGE

Monday he wakes me after he showers
with a hand on my stomach. He smells
like soap and coffee. Tuesday he cuts
the grass. I meet him at the door with water,
towel the sweat from his forehead.
On Wednesday we sit on the sofa,
my feet on his lap. We watch too many
hours of reality television, then go
to bed early. On Thursday, I show him
again the easiest way to chop an onion.
I make chicken soup, he cleans the dishes.
We fold laundry and play with our cats.
On Friday, we meet after work
for dinner. It is date night; we talk
about the week and plan our grocery list.
Saturday morning we sleep late. I indulge
myself in his warmth, feel protected
in his orbit. Then it is Sunday,
more chores around the house,
our schedules built to end the day
with *Desperate Housewives* and a plate
full of food, the same as every
other house on the block.

BEFORE THE REPEAL OF DADT

I'm tired of being a dancing queen,
marching in disco rhythm, carrying
your loaded guns, wiping your sweat,
putting on our pretty faces with rouge
and blood. We die, too, for freedom, for the sanctity
of countries who throw stones at swinging corpses.
We will lay down our bodies on your stiff-
spined backs to protect you from falling bombs
but you'd rather lose a limb
than hear a story about my husband?
Fuck you, America. Fuck your selective freedom
and your unprejudiced bullets of war.
Fuck our tender hearts for taking one
for the team, again and again. Fuck us
if we don't take our trigger fingers and replace them
with our middle fingers the next time
our squadrons are ambushed;
may we finally decide to man-up,
to demand, to tell.

WE LEFT EARLY

Boys, your beds are poison with flowers,
condom wrappers, you don't know why
you bother, but you do, some of you,
the sum of us who never
so much as cross our legs
in your twinkling little minds.

Young men: we are your elders,
your young grandfathers, old fathers,
your dusty uncles hanging around
the dustier backshelves of abandoned bookstores,
the years of decadence and ignorance,
the first toasts to freedom in the decade after blood.

We are the ghosts
of your closets full of envious clothes,
of your hallways full of friends who come
and go through us, the dancing specters
twirling pretty for impatient audiences
who never look up, who author ten-syllable

declarations of love with their horny little thumbs.
Do you pause for a moment, sensing we are here? Do you
tread on our beautiful shadows, never listening
when you ask questions aloud—*does he like me,
should I call him*—as we shout the affirmative
from where our lungs used to be?

The daisies wilted, the ones in the wine bottles,
the overpriced Riesling you drank
on the floor by the window when it snowed
and you kissed him for the second time. That
was a show. If you'd turned your ear,
we'd have told you he was sincere, whispered

through the radio a love song, something Diana Ross,
something gorgeous and lost, like us. But we're watching,
not as guides or guardian angels, just as boys once
and never again, once a boy, like you, just like you,

kissing dragons on the lips, walking planks,
only not living to tell the tale, not a click away,

not your gay ol' auntie Frank, not a hot cup of tea,
not Sunday champagne, not sewing that rip
in the seat of your pants. We would have done
these things. Patted your heads, offered our shoulders,
made you French toast with fruit and spotted you a ten
from our powdered bosom. Instead, we observe:

unnoticed. We speak in draft and creak,
a generation missing between generations,
the drawbridge between time, the comfort
of clean sheets waiting, the smell of men burning
in our fireplaces, the sight of wild roses
that hold their color against our lonely, lovely graves.

THE BOOK OF BRADLEY

I will never be a father or an older brother
but that day I was both, a high school junior
giving the keys to you, barely 13, barely tall enough

to see over the dash of my red Ford Mustang. You
would have been fine on those country backroads
had the sheriff not appeared in the rearview,

had you not lifted your foot and slowed to a crawl,
had you not been a highway toddler in irresponsible care,
then blue lights, of course, and we died together

as he walked to the driver's side, ticket pad in hand,
but when he saw you he laughed and said
don't let cops scare you, boy.

We tell this story over beers
on your 27th birthday. I am 31.
You have your beard and ambition. I have

my husband. I have never loved you more
than this moment. I have never better understood
what I've missed, what I've had.

WE PLANTED THESE TREES BY HAND

Dumbass 1 asks the questions
I hear most, *Which one is the woman?*
Which one do you call Ma?

I ask him back *Which one of your parents takes it
from behind?* Dumbasses 2 and 3 turn like wolves,
growling laughter. I get this, mostly from the guys,

girls, sometimes, too, when they travel
in packs and sharpen their teeth on anything
different: longer socks, new haircut, two dads.

I can see it in their eyes, though, jealous of my solid pair
to their awkward four, to their bickering three,
to their lonely one and weekend visitation; no stepmonsters

in my house, just footballs and violins, rooms full
of the smell of baking bread and used books. I can name
the last 20 Secretaries of State. My batting average

is .385. I know my home wasn't created
by a six-pack and a busted rubber. My folks
fought for me. *Who fought you into existence?*

HETERO

Brutality on the sidewalk!
You do not so much as hiss
today, theatre against the nights,
after your gym, your wife at home
with a migraine, you strip in my door,
enter my hungry spotlight, the director
who makes my love pathological.
There's the dishonest caressing of my hair,
the thieving tan hand, no decency
to remove the ring that is cold
on my forehead, so I growl, take the finger
in my mouth, consider, for a moment,
ripping it from the rest of you
with jealous teeth, jealous gums,
jealous lips that adore and curse you.
You make my love pathological.
Sometimes when I lean into you
I taste her, smell the afterbirth
of your sex, the happy miscarriages.
I think one of us
is schizophrenic. Surely we are mad
to roll like this together, gathering speed,
a boulder toward your
perfect house, your family,
your twin boys. Do they know
I swallow their siblings
were your deposit made
at the meeting of their mother's legs?
Last night you kissed me after,
a first, and then today,
my blood on the pavement,
bludgeoned with your silence,
strapping me in your anniversary gift,
a straight-
jacket. It is here I wait for you,
for us together in another life,
remembering too late
how you told me once
you don't believe in reincarnation.

MARK'S BIRTHDAY

After two pints of Guinness I announced
to the strangers and friends celebrating
Mark's birthday that my test came back

negative. The guys clapped and there were
high fives but one pulled me aside and asked
Would you have done the same if you were positive?

Ashamed through my buzz, I couldn't believe
I'd forgotten Austin and Tony and Dave. I couldn't
believe I'd walked into a room full of black men

and announced I was white, a room full of
Christians and announced I was atheist. I *do not*
see us as separate. I would kiss Tony on the lips

and have Dave in my home, but even these things
sound suspiciously similar to *I'm no racist;
I have Asian friends.* That night, at the table,

my relief was the sea that made us unequal.
I rode my own stupid waves of exoneration
from sexual ignorance to social bliss

and could not pretend the boys weren't drowning,
some of them. I was too quick to avoid hands
that could have pulled me in the poison;

just as thankful for forgiving friends
as I was for the dumb luck that accompanied
too many rubberless fucks.

NATIONAL COMING OUT DAY, 1998

As a sophomore I skipped my classes,
hid in my dorm-room closet, lived on warm soda

and stale crackers and pissed in a cup
instead of walking down the hallway

or across campus, instead of making
myself an easy target for sniper glances

as deadly as a hatchet to my Southern-Baptist
cock. For twelve hours of daylight,

I stood mute, a boy petrified
of the monsters under his creaking bed,

of judgmental angels with letterman jackets,
of firing squad congregations, without even

a glimmer in the warzone of a country boy's brain
that one day, I'd feel October on my shirtless skin.

MOTHER-IN-LAW

That first year, your mother was Debbie
from *Queer as Folk*. I couldn't
think of her otherwise, red-headed, brassy.

She would call
during every date. It
was a good son's duty to answer.

Once, when you weren't looking,
I turned off your phone. An hour later,
she knocked on our door.

I invited her in for breakfast
and began the balancing act
every man has to learn.

THE BOOK OF DMITRI

To call it a book is a misnomer,
more like a trashy romance novella
we all read on park benches
then hid in our designer man-bags
when we'd return from trick lunches.
This is what I remember
of Dmitri, what we all remember
of Dmitri: we fell for his thick
accent, the *no?* he'd kiss gently
onto every sentence. We told our
girlfriends about his traveling tongue,
took pleasure in their jealousy
as it spread like communism
over the Eastern European maps
we unfolded in public libraries
just to appear knowledgeable
of his geography. We swooned
when he promised to take us
to Pitsunda, the place he described
as paradise, then swallowed him
at his strong tsar-command
like the vodka shots every bartender
gave him for free. When acquaintances
peppered their sentences
with Russian words, we shook off
any thought of coincidence. Surely
there was more than one
young homosexual named Dmitri
in Little Rock, Arkansas,
who taught Southern boys like us
to say *Pah-ka, moya lee-u-bov.*

HALINEN
JEREMY

prodigal songs

Jeremy Halinen co-edits *Knockout Literary Magazine*. *What Other Choice*, his first full-length collection of poems, won the 2010 Exquisite Disarray First Book Poetry Contest and is available online at alibris.com. His poems have also appeared in *Best Gay Poetry 2008*, the *Los Angeles Review*, *Poet Lore*, *Sentence*, and elsewhere. He resides in Seattle.

www.knockoutlit.org

Jeremy Halinen

FOR MY STRAIGHT BROTHERS CONSIDERING

when you come inside her with a moan
you forget
where you have come from
and where you are going
doesn't matter

think of the first raindrop
hitting earth
oh drop what did you win
you were the first
to disappear

MEETING HIS PARENTS

When they asked me how
we met and I told them
after bringing him home

and fucking him that night
I pried his mouth open
with a kiss

and ejaculated into his throat
as he tried, like a good trick,
not to gag but failed

and curled like a child
homesick for his mother's womb,
they swallowed—

perhaps thinking of how roughly
they fucked each other
when they were young—

and stared at my tongue
as if hoping to find,
instead of rooted muscle,

it was a scarf
they could pull out of me
like a magic trick

to wrap around my neck.

SNOW

I wake and find a light dusting
fell in me while I slept.

He is with me in   my bed,
his breath hot on   my neck,
his naked body clutching   me.
I do not like it. I have not
for so long, though I have tried, believe me,
that I cannot remember
what it is to be a sandcastle on a beach without a rising tide.

In the shower, because I have to, I disregard the years,
               I tell him   he must leave me,
I tell him   I'll take him anywhere he wants to go
but when we get there   I will leave him

                  because I have to.
I hold his face under the showerhead
so he appears to be crying more than he can,
because otherwise   he will not believe me.

Jeremy Halinen

THOSE LIGHTS IN MY EYES ARE SCARS

Liking men is
like walking barefoot
an underwater tightrope
and looking up
through sinking spears
of filtered light,
thinking not of what
can't be seen
but of oxygen
too far to inhale.
Yet when I take them
inside me, I feel
real, and after,
miss more
than I intend.

MAKE WAY FOR FUCKLING

The glass prison down the street
held my vision. I was too young

to cum, but that did not edge

my desire. I pledged to sell my
virgin ass to the highest bidder,

but every time I sashayed past,

the light refracted by the walls
obscured the twinkles trying

to reach me from inmates' eyes.

The devil said, no matter the price,
he'd never sell his soul to a man.

But for a child? Would any man

lay his cock on the block for me?
I wanted to see, I needed to feel

his embrace a loose noose tightening.

BEAUTIFUL BAREBACK

We're making a scene,
one men destined to die
have acted out for millennia,
you'll soon forget,
but now, watching us,
you leak, wet, don't you,
into your palm. We're not
done yet, a sword
pulled halfway from its sheath,
then re-sheathed,
again and again,
as if the mind
that controls the hand
that holds the handle
can't decide
whether to fight
or flee. It's free for you
to watch us on your screen.

ERECTION DAY

God is not smart, clearly—
consider these sails, gaudy,
at full mast in a still wind
that doesn't blow—well,
anywhere we need to go.
Notice, also, no ships here
in the harbor, just prodigal
songs spilling from the tips
of spears like mutant tears
of paradise. His will is dumb.
His kingdom, cum: on earth,
some sort of heaven.

SHADOW OF METH

You're riding him bareback
fifteen yards from tracks
in a hard rain, hair dripping.
The train nears; you sense
he's about to come.
He appears to be crying,
but it's likely just rain.
His rhythm synchs
with the train's. In passing,
wheels fling from the track
a scrap of metal, which slices
through your neck as the train
blows its whistle, your trick
his load, and you yours.
Your head falls toward his.
Within seconds, he seems
to be crying blood,
but it's yours.

FRANK 3
for CA Conrad

both of frank's eyeballs
are pregnant with twins
he wonders when
the small new eyes
will see
and what

where they'll sit
when the old eyes split
and how they'll sew
the old ones shut

will they fit him
for two more pairs of glasses
or just one special new pair
that corrects all six eyes
called whyfocals

if he wakes as a child one day
what names will they call him
at school

FRANK 4
for CA Conrad

frank woke from his sunday afternoon nap
with assholes for eyes
and shit for brains

he groped his way to the kitchen

you should have gone to church with me
his wife scolded
clearly, god is punishing you
but she gave him a laxative
and led him to the toilet

i don't care if this is the eleventh plague
frank said
as he waited for peristalsis
to clear his mind
i'll never go to church again
god can kiss my eyes!

after he finished
he wiped both holes at once
with four squares of toilet paper
bunched in each hand
did i miss a spot?
he asked his wife

she plucked a speck
of toilet paper from the edge
of his right eyehole
and kissed him on the cheek

if you rim them
you'll make it into guinness
he said

if only i had two tongues
she said
slipping two fingers
deep into his head
like thoughts

ANTLER

poetry sucks

Antler, author of the Ginsberg-praised epic poem "Factory," has published work in hundreds of periodicals, including *City Lights Review*, *New Directions Journal*, *Whole Earth Review*, *Earth First! Journal*, *Exquisite Corpse*, *Kenyon Review*, and *Chiron Review*. His poem "Somewhere Along the Line," published in *The Sun*, was awarded a 1993 Pushcart Prize. His poems have also appeared in dozens of anthologies, including *Erotic by Nature*, *Son of the Male Muse*, *Earth Prayers*, and *A Day for a Lay: A Century of Gay Poetry*. He has taught at Esalen Institute in California, Omega Institute of New York, Antioch College in Ohio, and the Kerouac Poetics School in Boulder. He has performed his poetry at Wilderness University, the Sigurd Olson Environmental Institute, Sarah Lawrence College, the International Festival of the Poet in Rome, New York City's Museum of Modern Art, and many other places.

www.antlerpoet.net

"POETRY SUCKS!"

The word "sucks" is being abused
   by being used
      derogatorily.
The word "sucks" molested by youths
   under the age of consent
      insulting
Poetry and babies and cocksuckers alike
   not to mention adult titsuckers,
      tongue-suckers, thumb-suckers, toe-suckers
   nose and earlobe-suckers, sucker suckers
      and trees who suck the earth
   and butterflies who suck flowers
      and black holes who suck galaxies.
Like it or not, boys in every state of America
   in every city every town
      when poetry is mentioned
   say "Poetry sucks!"
Cute youths who never get sucked
   and have no inkling of blowjobjoy
      taking advantage of
   the word "sucks"
      putting poetry down—
True, poetry sucks, but not derogatorily.
Poetry sucks beautifully, beautiful
   as a blowjob tongue swirling
      round the most sensitive spots.
And guess what?
Every day poets all over Earth
   compose thousands of brand-new
      100% guaranteed cocksucking hymns
   that swell the accumulated
      immortal poetry of the ages.
Yeah, Poetry sucks: Poetry exposes itself
   to punks who sneer "Poetry sucks!"
      in the image of a big blowjob
   that gives them instantaneous hardons
      that won't be satisfied
till they get their first suck.
No problem.

Enough poets exist—men, boys, women, girls—
    to help out.
Give a blowjob to every boy who says
    "Poetry sucks!"
Simple as that.

JACK OFF SÉANCE

Those who want to communicate
    with their lost loved ones
Should gather around a boy's stiff cock
    more than any crystal ball.
Jack off séance—a boy's big boner
    illuminated in a dark room,
The guests in a circle around him,
    each gets his change
    to hold the stiff prick
    and ask it a question.
The answer is in the throbs.
One throb means yes.
Two throbs mean yes.
A boy's full-fledged erection
    is more a medium, more a fortune-teller
    than the most authentic gypsy.
The answer is in the spurts.
To make a boy's cock spurt
    is to make all the dead speak
    in the most beautiful way they could.

WRITERS WORKSHOP

At last in the clearing in the hot afternoon sun
    amid thousands of flies and wasps
The four dead soldiers were found by their comrades,
    naked, twisted, mutilated—
One with his hands and feet cut off,
    the cut-off feet placed where the hands were,
        the cut-off hands placed where the feet were;
Another with brains scooped out and placed in two piles
    on the chest like breasts
        with a gouged-out eye on top of each;
Another, a young woman with her eyes missing
    later found stuffed up her vagina
        and the genitals of her companions
    crammed in her mouth;
The last, a mere boy, disemboweled, decapitated
    with the guts placed where the head was
        and the buttocks cut off to the bone
    and placed over the face
        with the cut-off nose and tongue
    stuck up the asshole.
Meanwhile, on another continent,
    in an air-conditioned
        university building
A creative writing class listens
    to the poet-professor explain why
        political poetry is not
    poetry but rants
        disguised as poetry
And assigns them to write
    for next class poems
        about their grandmothers.

MILITARY RECRUITERS VS. GAY-LOVE RECRUITERS

Military recruiters can address
   high school boys in the classroom
To seduce them to become
   skilled killers
But gay-love recruiters can't address
   boys in the classroom
To seduce them to delight
   in same-sex love.
Military recruiters can show boys
   films of victorious battles.
Gay love recruiters can't show boys
   films of visionary gay sex.
And of course uniformed killers
   are heroes
While young men who love
   sucking teenage boys' cocks with love
     are child molesters,
Besides, there's no need for homosexuals to recruit—
Every boy who loves playing with his cock
   loves playing with a boy's cock.
Even the boy who claims he doesn't have
   a gay bone in his body
     loves watching his own cock come.

FIRING SQUAD VS. JACK OFF SQUAD

Rather than blow taps over dead soldiers
    in coffins with flags draped o'er them,
        blow taps o'er live soldiers in uniform
    who never killed anyone
        getting blowjobs from live soldiers in uniform
    who never killed anyone
        and wipe there sucked off cocks with our flag.
How beautiful the young soldiers are in uniform
    with their erections sticking out
        serviced by our young recruits in uniform
    on their knees.
How beautiful to see our flag
    being used to wipe the lips
        of our devout cocksuckers in uniform
    and the ecstatic cocks fulfilling their duty
        to God and their country!
And instead of a firing squad,
    firing their rifles at the clouds
        at the end of the ceremony,
    as the coffin lid is closed
        and the coffin is lowered into the Earth,
A jack off squad of young recruits
    who never killed anyone
        jacking off toward the clouds
    at the end of the ceremony
        as the coffin is unearthed and opened
    and the corpse rises and comes back to life!

DOG LICKING BOY'S FACE VS. PRIEST LICKING BOY'S FACE

OK for cute healthy dog
    to run up to a strange boy
        with playful joy
    and leap up
        and lick the boy's face
But not OK for a priest
    respected by the whole community
        to run up to a boy he doesn't know
    get on his knees and pant
        and whimper
    and leap up
        and lick his nose, cheeks, face.

If dogs can get away with licking
    teenage boys' beautiful faces
        why not a priest?
You mean it's legal for a dog
    to tongue-kiss a boy's face
        and not a priest—
a priest who is a go-between
    between you and Almighty God?
Shouldn't people regard a priest
    acting like an affectionate puppy
        to a cute boy he never saw before
just as appropriate and charming?

And if a boy thinks nothing
    of letting the dog see and smell and lick
        his genitals now and then in secret
and he tells no one
    why can't a youth think nothing
of letting his favorite priest
    get a chance
to see what a boy's cock is like
    seeing as the priest's boyhood cock
has already ascended to Heaven?

For the youth thinks,
    doesn't his boyhood body and soul
        go to Heaven long before
    the man dies
        so it can greet him there
    like a puppy
        when the time comes?

BOY TALKING IN HIS SLEEP

My friend's boner is a puppy
    that follows me home from school
        and won't take no for an answer.
My friend's cock getting hard is a kitten
    that purrs when I pet it
        and won't take no for an answer.
My friend's dick spurting is more fun
    that my pet frog's tongue
        leaping out of its mouth to catch a dragonfly
            then leaping back in again.
My pal's wiener is more fun that a firefly
    captured in a bottle next to my bed at night
        because just licking my pal's nipples lightly
            makes him come.
My chum's hotdog smells better than my pet snake
    and doesn't have to be fed mice
        and smells better than my pet toad
            and doesn't have to be fed crickets
                and is cuter
            when its engorged glans
        emerge from its prepuce than my pet turtle's head
    emerging from its shell.
My best buddy's pud turns me into a dog
    begging at the table for a bone
        and drooling while the family laughs
            and then the father throws it to me
        and if you try taking it from me I growl.
My bestfriend's donkeykong is more fun than Old Faithful
    not because it spurts on the hour every hour
        which it does every day every week every month every year
            but because you can eat every spurt
                and lick up the drops
            with light-licking tongue-licks
        that make his silky belly quiver
    while his peter gets hard again.
Yeah, my best pal's lollapallooza refuses to let me do my homework
    till it's tickled my tonsils which are jealous
        they aren't his balls but when he ejaculates
            are delighted to be frosted with his sperm

    like two snowballs
     we added to the giant snowcock
   we made in the park
  after the blizzard.
Yeah, my boyfriend metronoming his hardon
  from side-to-side in front of my face
    hypnotized me to do its bidding
      its wish is my command—
       if 3 times a night it requires
     my mouth be a pussy he fucks so be it
   if 3 times a night it must go spelunking
up my hinder so be it
   if 3 times a night it must be petted
     with the inside of my fur-lined glove
      its entire length and circumference
    before being milked so be it
  it won't take no for an answer.
Yeah, my bosom-buddy's kaleidoscope is so cute
  kids with no pubic hair
    pay a dollar to see it
     2 dollars to watch it get hard
      3 dollars to touch it
     4 dollars to put the ruby tip in their mouth
   while looking wistfully
  in his sky-blue eyes.
Hey man, mi amigo as a gesture of thanks and affection
  lightly caresses my eyes and nose and lips as I sleep
    with his erection
     so I wake in my dream
    as he jacks off in my face smiling
 as I look at him with total awe and devotion.

STANDS TO REASON

If when 20, 14-year-old boys seemed cute to you,
If at 40, 20-year-olds seemed cute to you,
If at 60, 40-year-old men seemed cute to you,
If at 80, 60-year-old men seemed cute to you,
If at 100, 80-year-old men seemed cute to you,
If as a just-dead corpse, 100-year-old men
    seemed cute to you,
If as a just-defleshed white skeleton,
    rotting corpses seemed cute to you,
If as a disintegrating white skeleton,
    just-defleshed white skeletons seemed cute to you,
If as a skeleton turned to dust,
    disintegrating white skeletons seemed cute to you,
If as dust in smaller particles from skeletons turned to dust,
    larger particles of dust from skeletons turned to dust
        seemed cute to you,
So—What next?
Molecules of memories of desire
Reflect light clinging to dust motes
    floating in shafts of sunlight
        in abandoned attics
    in abandoned old farmhouses
        till dust mites magnified 10,000 times
    devour dust motes for dinner
While pure nothingness longs for
Rotting human corpsefleshsmell
Like a 14-year-old boy in awe
    of his bestfriend's hairless armpit aroma
        on a summer afternoon
    wondering if he eats his own semen
        when he jacks off
    will he be immortal?

WHEN NO ONE'S LOOKING

Rather than become friends with boys
   become friends with photos of boys
      when no one's looking.
Rather than kiss a boy
   kiss a statue of a boy
      when no one's looking.
Rather than caress a boy's hair
   caress the grass over a boy's grave
      when no one's looking.
Rather than sleep next to a naked boy
   sleep next to a book of poems about
      sleeping next to naked boys
when no one's looking.
Rather than jack off a boy
   jack off yourself
      looking at photos of yourself
as a boy
   who no longer exists
and if he did would find it
   hard to believe he became you.
Rather than blow a boy
   drink the imagined reflection
      of his erection
in the pond in the mind
   miles from nowhere.
Why not sense the soft spring breeze
   that smells so good
      is the smell
   of silken boy armpits
      wafted nostrilward
   from the utopias to be
      after the utopia America becomes
a thousand years from now
   crumbles to dust when no one's looking.
Who needs living boys anyway
   when all the dead and unborn boys
      are so lonely
   for a boy-loving man's maternal regard?

Climb wild mountains to their peaks
    and speak to the boys of the past
        and the boys of the future
    who understand your longing and vision
        better than any living boy
    when no one's looking.
They never let you down, they never grow old,
    they love you with boyish love
        forever when no one's looking.
Why not embrace your death
    as if it's the most beautiful youth
        who love you
    and will be your young pal forever
        in the big mystery
    of whatever happens
        when no one's looking.

HER LAST SUMMER

The old mare knows
    this is her last summer
        and spends her days
    in the pasture
with the two fillies
    who like each other
        and doze
standing side-by-side
    in opposite directions
        with their heads
    on each other's rumps.

FRANCO
JAMES
poems inspired by

Frank J Miles writes of **James Franco**: I will go Ms. Jenkins on anyone hating. Mr. James Franco is the Quintessential Artpomo of Our Time. He was the kid that stole everyone's hat on the playground, not the one off to the side eating paste. He's not humorless or self-serious. And what makes him great rather than, say, awesome: His unquenchable curiosity. His ambition for productivity and its achievement. An acute awareness of mortality; therefore, a terror about sleep because he has too much to do before death—signs of genius. And he likes bears (Google it—Image Search).

www.whosay.com/jamesfranco

JAMES FRANCO
by Alex Dimitrov

I would sleep with James Franco as Allen Ginsberg
and Allen Ginsberg would sleep with James Franco
as James Dean. Woof, woof and a howl.
James Franco makes me growl.

At the office I think about James Franco
as more than just performance art.
At my desk and in my poems—
I take him seriously, I write into him real hard.

Woof, woof and a howl.
I even like to watch James Franco scowl.
Once at a New York loft party a famous poet said,
"You are your author photo."

James Franco, James Franco, I love you.

DREAMING OF JAMES FRANCO
by Stephen Scott Mills

Sometimes he's a poet, jittery and full of coffee and cigarettes
        and long lines that wrap around my back and up between
my legs where he likes to spend his afternoons.
        He believes we are the best minds of our generation
and who is going to argue with that?

Other times he comes to me with his boyish charm, messy hair,
        and perfect skin. He's a freak to my geek.
He listens to The Who. I unbutton his pants. He pretends
        to not notice as I take him in my mouth and show him
all the ways to survive the coming decades. For I know a thing
        or two about the Midwest in the 1980s.

One night he's an activist, mustached and growing tired
        of the fight. We drink milk in bed with his naked
thigh pressing against mine. When we wake, someone has died.
        Everything is silent. Nothing is the same.
We don't make love again.

Once in awhile he's just a rich kid avenging his father's death.
        Spouting out lines of cheesy dialogue, but always
with that brooding face. He presses me against his desk,
        asks about my fear of spiders. Then he enters me.
Tells me I'll learn to like it. *Don't be afraid.*

Tonight he is just James. A grad student who likes to talk
        lit theory while I stroke his cock.
There's empty wine bottles on the floor, which I have drunk.
        Jimmy don't drink. He gives me that goofy smile
and I'm all his until morning when I'm back here in bed with you.

@JAMESFRANCO
by Sam W. Sanders

a life glimpsed
through the nonsense of short urls
to electronic destinations
stark in color and expression

an external identity cultivated
through multiple mediums.
letters. gestures. blurry video.
a family freely shared.
a face poured into the world
from an angular smile
under a skewed coif

a calque of self to social feeds,
that life's one big art scene.

it is the little things running
oblique to your internalization
of the figure towering on screen
that confuses you.

remember, the unscripted celebrity is licensed to strange.

you can pretend to know a man
but you only know what he allows you to see

RANDOM WORDS
by Bradley Bentz

on a cold rainy day outside
the san francisco train co.
strolls james franco wearing a raincoat,
escaping the stress of sounds
that success made with pineapple express.
forgetting he was once a hard fighting seaman,
before he was the weedman,
he played a 1950's rebel without a cause,
james dean man.
he may be a freak and even a geek,
ivy league educated (ivy leaf medicated?),
knowing whatever it takes, and at any cost,
he walks through the valley of elah with a full glass of milk.
jilted by the good times, maxed out by love and distrust,
always sonny in disposition.
throwing up wild deuce peace signs,
that's usually an all american culture crime,
all the time thinking about the dead girl
127 hours after his date night.
he howls obscenities about revolution,
muttering about shadows and lies and great raids
with people acting in ape ways.
while he may just be james franco, in a raincoat,
strolling outside the san francisco train co.,
remember he's in the same boat as plain folk
acting out his part in life.

OK, SO I MET JAMES FRANCO
by Perry Brass

OK, so I met James Franco
at Yale, and I was forty years
younger—only 23—and he bumped
                        into me
on purpose because I was so attractive
and magnetic and alive that he couldn't
ignore me under his Hollywood shades
and hoodie and pretend
that he was disappearing
into regular graduate studenthood,
and we went back to his "rooms"

and made love to Berlioz on his sound system
because he wanted to impress me—
                        a bit,
and himself too, and afterwards
he explained to me that he would love
to walk holding hands with me
                        through the Quads,
but it would be on Facebook in a minute,
and he was captured by his ambition,
a pawn of his history, extradited
to the land of the Famous trying
to be normal while selling their souls
to Mammon, and I smiled. And he smiled back,
with his gentle radiance that could not be
                        captured
or extradited, or released to anyone
except to me, at that moment, in that clear
window of words that we both used
to see each other with.

Dec. 4, 2011
train into New York.
Note: James Franco is a graduate student in English at Yale.
Extra note: I have never met him.

A POEM FOR JAMES FRANCO
by Shane Allison

James Franco understands the human heart
  I wish James Franco ruled the world
Because of James Franco, I stay off the wrong side of the tracks
  I run my fingers through James Franco's curly hair
James Franco says I could sleep in the basement
  I cry because James Franco cries, too
I touch myself when thinking of James Franco wandering inside me
  James Franco is surrounded by flowers
I touch my lips when I see James Franco
  I drink the Kool-Aid James Franco gives me for my bronchitis
I imagine James Franco writing poems about me while in his underwear
  I am the man of the house when James Franco is gone
James Franco brainwashed me into believing that I'm a platypus
  I smell James Franco's freshly baked cherry pies
I wish James Franco would stop cheating off my math test
  My mother is having James Franco over for dinner
James Franco can read my thoughts
  Without James Franco things are sour and bitter
I hear James Franco rummaging around in my refrigerator
  Wish I could speak a little more like James Franco
I see and remember James Franco
  Because of James Franco, I am a poet
I imagine James Franco standing on snow-capped mountains
  I say there is someone else, and his name is James Franco
I don't love you the way I love James Franco
  I feel this wall separating me and James Franco
Don't you love this mink coat James Franco bought me
  I wish I was James Franco
I say things no one else understands except James Franco
  Imagine James Franco wearing a pink bunny suit
I hope James Franco will come to my house and play Yahtzee with me
  I see James Franco in the fog of Manhattan
I wonder if James Franco knows if I will ever get married
  I see James Franco looking back at me in the mirror
James Franco invited me to stay the week at his condo in Aspen

RIVER, RUN
By Luke Shearfrond

River, run.

River, meet me in Palo Alto.

In my mind's eye,
I see you, smoking a cigarette
you're as high as my soaring spirits
wearing a leather jacket
nothing else.

Harry, here.

Harry, hand me over that cigarette.

My Renaissance Man,
I scrap each dripping word
that falls from your succulent prose
and each tender color
relish like a love letter.

Saul, smile.

Saul, brush my cheek with your hand.

I imagine kissing you,
my bum unshaven cheeks
scraping gently against your manly ruggedness
and the longing is unbearable.

James, meet me in Palo Alto.
Where the wind whispers on our shoulders.
And the buildings are the color of shadows.

LEARNING THROUGH OSMOSIS: ASLEEP AT COLUMBIA UNIVERSITY
By Jory Mickelson

[Never Been Kissed]
It is important to remember when we begin
any endeavor, it is that, a beginning. No one
can recall your face, because it is the first time
anyone has seen it—a first kiss for the eye.

[Freaks and Geeks]
You were trying to teach all of us how to be
the worst kind of student. Skinny and greasy
with your gigantic mouth, it isn't enough
to be in band, but you have to be in a band.

[Spiderman]
We all want to be the hero in the story, with
or without red tights. The hard fact is that not all
of us have what it takes, a dimpled chin perhaps.
Instead, we become sidekicks, the odd man out.

[Herbert White]
Sometimes a movie becomes a poem for the eye. The violent race
of frames pile up like innumerable bodies, leaving the audience
reeling, transfixed by every shaky angle. The lull of the theater,
a dark forest, and the screen, the white sawing static of the sun.

[James Dean]
This is where you learn to love smoking, never
touching them and then blowing through two packs
a day. You teach yourself what it is to be an icon,
isolate for three months, turn your life to ash.

[Annapolis]
Only so many are deemed worthy to pass through
the gates. Sometimes to get ahead, you need to learn
how to box. In the ring, if you pay attention you will
begin to see something of yourself in your opponent.

[Howl]
How I love you in those horn-rims. Let me pay homage to how
hot you looked. I think my obsession with your eyewear may be
considered obscene, but I don't care, I have to say it. There is no
way round the way you turn my stomach upside-down as Ginsberg.

[The Wicker Man]
What does it mean to get the last word in a film
or to appear in the final scene? One gets almost
no credit; even though your dialogue could imply
a sequel, even though you give it your all.

[Candy Magazine]
Trans-formation takes great effort. It's impossible to change
without the right tools. What are you offering to help us
overcome our bad habits, our static lives? Blue eye shadow,
black leather gloves, red bowed lips and your onyx heart.

[Date Night]
It's cliché to say that home is where the heart is,
but I have reservations about doing away with
the well-worn phrase. What can take its place?
All else seems counterfeit, a rose by another name.

[Milk]
Sometimes I wonder what it would be like to kiss Sean Penn.
I could ask Madonna of course, or Susan Sarandon, Jewel or
Scarlett Johansen, but you know too. Would he complain
about the way my mustache scratched him after our lips met?

[The Feast of Stephen]
We always judge ourselves against the appearance of others.
How do we measure up against the next man? As if looking
good was a kind of competitive sport for one-person teams.
We spend hours at the gym and even there, eye the competition.

[SNL: Lawrence Welk Skit]
Life will meet our expectations about three out of every four
times. We spend three-quarters of our lives awake and seventy-
five percent of our waking day at work. One quarter of the time,
if we are awake life surprises us—snow in June. Junice.

[Palo Alto]
Take heed, not everything works out. There is a point
at which you find a need to turn around. I don't know exactly
what I'm saying here. The way a T-ball coach tells you,
Good effort when you don't make a single base.

[The Green Hornet]
We often make friends with the people from our first job, even if
we don't keep it for the rest of our lives. If I took another job,
I would hope to keep the friends that I had made. I would hope
they'd continue to pop by, even if just for a quick hello.

[Eat Pray Love]
You teach us it's okay make the wrong decision, even though
we don't know it's wrong at the time because it feels so good.
The way we can date the same person over and over, each
with a different name and never know why the breakup comes.

[Knocked Up]
If you ask the right kind of questions, you are going to get
answers. You might not like some of those answers, but
they are going to be important, maybe information you've
never considered. Be careful what you go asking for.

[Gucci]
What kind of smell are you selling? Is it the scent of cotton,
wet from the chlorinated pool? Is it the fragrance of your
perfectly waxed arms that lift you like Botticelli's Venus?
In this black and white billboard ad, there are so many grays.

[Oscar Host]
Sometimes we feel a need to insert ourselves into another's
story. How far will each of us go to bump up next to someone
else at a party? We try to find a balance between nonchalance
and showing up in the other person's dress and heels.

[127 Hours]
If I could spend a little more than five days with you, I know you'd come
around to my way of thinking. I'd give you seven thousand six-hundred,
twenty reasons for my cause. After four hundred fifty-seven thousand,
two-hundred seconds together, you couldn't resist saying yes, yes.

JAMES FRANCO'S DIFFERENT SEXIES
by Ed Rose

Sometimes I find James Franco sexy
in a completely face-related way.
Jawlines, pulling up into
classic electroshock hair, wide electroshock eyes
and bristles of lash linings
His lines. His lines are sexy.
I want to take a Cannon like a hipster kid
and a snap away,
maybe just
just touching his chin
when I move it, like crystals in light.
I find him sexy in line and figure some days.
Some other days
that's not exactly
my first thought.
maybe,
just maybe,
a different
cannon
touch
bristling
snap
hard move
electroshock.

ALLEN AT THE OSCARS
by Philip Clark

Everyone wonders what was wrong
With James Franco at the Oscars:
Such hardness in his eyes, mouth
A marble line—while Ms. Hathaway,
All teeth and gleam, rabbited
Around the stage, expending
Energy for two.
                          But no wonder.
Few had seen Franco-as-Ginsberg
In that recent film, and not the Hare
Krishna Allen, not the sweet
Old man, belly of Buddha, darling
Of the college circuit. My roommate
Saw him in that stage, at Radford U,
Rural Virginia, when he'd take any gig
Where the closeted boys could come
Sit at his feet, soak in the legend.
But James played early Allen, Allen in
Those photos at the National Gallery:
Snapshots from the cold-water flats,
Overcoat hunched against the rooftop
Gales, when thirty bucks a month was rent
And the El's ceaseless rattle matched
Subways below crumbled streets.
                          No wonder
In that crowd of gowns, paparazzi
Flashbulb pops and banks of microphones,
He stood on stage, empty-eyed,
Skipped the celebrations, hopped a red-eye
Flight across country, the plane's
Engines howling down a wide runway.

About the Cover Artist

HENSLEE
CODY

spencer

Cody Henslee, whose photograph, "Spencer," is featured on the cover of this issue of *Assaracus*, is working towards his BA in Art History with a minor in Photography at the University of Arkansas at Little Rock, where he lives. His ambition is to acquire his MFA in Photography and use his knowledge of art history to better inform his continuing body of work. His series, "With the Same Brush," of which "Spencer" is a part, deals with identity and one's loss of identity due to external presumptions about character. The model is Spencer Smith, also of Little Rock.

www.facebook.com/suffer4fashion

SUBMIT TO ASSARACUS

The mission of Sibling Rivalry Press is to develop, publish, and promote outlaw artistic talent—those projects which inspire people to read, challenge, and ponder the complexities of life in dark rooms, under blankets by cell-phone illumination, in the backseats of cars, and on spring-day park benches next to people reading Wilde and Crane. We encourage submissions to *Assaracus* by gay male poets of any age, regardless of background, education, or level of publication experience. Submissions are accepted during the months of January, May, and September. For more information, visit us online.

www.siblingrivalrypress.com